Work

What is Political Economy? series

Bruce Pietrykowski, *Work*

Work

Bruce Pietrykowski

polity

First published in 2019 by Polity Press

Polity Press
65 Bridge Street
Cambridge CB2 1UR, UK

Polity Press
101 Station Landing
Suite 300
Medford, MA 02155, USA

ISBN-13: 978-1-5095-3083-0
ISBN-13: 978-1-5095-3084-7 (pb)

A catalogue record for this book is available from the British Library.

Library of Congress Cataloging-in-Publication Data

Names: Pietrykowski, Bruce, author.
Title: Work / Bruce Pietrykowski.
Description: Medford, MA : Polity, 2019. | Series: What is political economy? | Includes bibliographical references and index.
Identifiers: LCCN 2018041115 (print) | LCCN 2018052080 (ebook) | ISBN 9781509530861 (Epub) | ISBN 9781509530830 (hardback) | ISBN 9781509530847 (paperback)
Subjects: LCSH: Work. | Equality. | Income distribution. | Economic policy. | BISAC: POLITICAL SCIENCE / Public Policy / Economic Policy.
Classification: LCC HD4904 (ebook) | LCC HD4904 .P54 2019 (print) | DDC 331–dc23
LC record available at https://lccn.loc.gov/2018041115

Typeset in 10.5 on 12 pt Sabon by Toppan Best-set Premedia Limited
Printed and bound in Great Britain by TJ International Limited

For further information on Polity, visit our website: politybooks.com

To my father, whose working life was devoted to promoting fair labor standards, preventing child labor and prosecuting wage theft.

Contents

1

Introduction: The Unique Character of Work

Work: A Political Economy Perspective

What is work and who (or what) works? Work is a special topic in political economy because it is integral to the production of valuable goods and services that we all use. The products of work may result in socially useful goods and services such as satisfying, nutritious meals and better health care. On the other hand, work may produce socially destructive products like weapons of mass destruction. While we would like to live in a world with more of the former and far fewer, preferably none, of the latter, they both entail the expenditure of effort. The way in which work is organized, the characteristics of workers and the compensation received from going to work is what this book is all about. As you can imagine, economists do not agree on what is most important about work, what to focus on, what to minimize and what is the best way to explain some of the most pressing issues associated with working. So this book will help to identify important debates over the nature of work, ranging from the problems of growing income inequality and the threat of technological unemployment to the future of work in a post-capitalist world.

Another goal of this book is to explore the nature of work from the perspective of political economy. The political economy approach – also referred to as heterodox economics

– is broadly identified by its commitment to a progressive, worker-centered vision of economic development. It draws on the traditions of Marx, Keynes, feminism and institutionalism as interpreted by contemporary economic theorists. The standpoint of heterodox political economy lies in opposition to the mainstream neoclassical, neoliberal economics found in most undergraduate textbooks and in appeals to free-market economic policies. Mainstream, neoclassical economics rests on a vision of an ideal economy characterized by individual self-interest, profit maximization and ruthless competition. By contrast, the political economy approach understands the lived experience of workers in a capitalist regime characterized by conflict, power and inequality. In addition, it is important to recognize that these forces are embedded in social norms – about gender roles, for example – and institutions – the state, for instance – that influence the distribution of workers to jobs and wages to workers.

Political economy differs from mainstream economics in a number of other important ways. First, it is political in a dual sense. It understands that access to and distribution of economic resources are the outcomes of power struggles involving groups defined by class, race, gender and location. In addition, political economy is associated with explicit values and norms such as the democratic control of economic institutions, the equitable distribution of economic resources, and the organization of an economy that meets human needs and develops the capacity for people to lead a meaningful life. It also recognizes that all economic paradigms – ways of making sense of the world – represent particular interests and values. There is no such thing as an objective, value-free economics (Stilwell 2016). Another feature of political economy that sets it apart from the mainstream is its focus on the historical development of contemporary economic life. That means that we cannot figure out where we are without analyzing where we have been and what forces were at play to get us to this point. History matters because it helps us to critically evaluate the present and future of work. In addition, the political economy approach is diverse, representing an array of different lenses through which to understand the economy. As a result, in contrast to the model of perfect competition in which power is an anomaly or a sign of market imperfection, the political economy approach incorporates power, conflict, control, resistance, cooperation and solidarity into the analysis of work.

But before we jump into an exploration of the political economy of work, we need to establish some boundaries on whose work we will be analyzing. This may at first seem like a simple matter. We will be discussing my work, your work, the work of humans in particular historical circumstances, right? Well, if work is the expenditure of productive effort, should we include non-human workers in the discussion? Animals have been used as workers for centuries, not only in agriculture – oxen or mules plowing fields – but also in manufacturing – horses used in textile manufacturing to power spinning machines – and in services – buggy rides and the nineteenth-century horse-drawn mass transit vehicle, the omnibus (see Text box 1.1). At the other end of the spectrum,

---

Text box 1.1 Are animals a part of the working class? Do fish resist?

There is a lively discussion, far removed from the debates in political economy, about the boundaries we draw between human and non-human participants in the economy. Jason Hribal provocatively argues that animals have been intimately involved in the making of the capitalist economy. Horses and oxen operated spinning machines and grinding stones. Horses are workers, but are they comparable to human workers? Their efforts certainly produce value for their employers. But do they have what social scientists call *agency* – the capacity to act intentionally, to plan, to choose, to resist? Writing a history of the horse's contribution to industrialization, Ann Norton Greene thinks not: "Clearly, it is inappropriate to impose a model of human agency upon another species, about whose cognition and consciousness we inevitably understand very little" (2008, 8). And yet, throughout her narrative, she consistently refers to horses as workers.

Marx distinguished animals from humans by noting that animals instinctively focus on their own immediate survival, whereas humans can plan and create alternative futures with their labor. This relegates animals to the realm of natural resources

Continued

Text box 1.1 (*Continued*)

to be used as their owners see fit. But can animals resist their fate? Historians and sociologists of animal studies think they can. Indeed, the traces of animal resistance are found in the very technologies deployed to capture and control them. Docile agricultural critters were made to be compliant. Investments in technology were made to keep creatures from escaping their fate as commodities to be trapped, bought, sold and consumed (Hribal 2003; Wadiwel 2016). The working dog breeds are examples of animals specifically bred to herd, transport and protect. As herders, for example, these dogs were "biotechnologies in a system of market farming that became contemporary capital-intensive agribusiness ... " (Haraway 2007, 56). So, while most research in the political economy of work focuses on human agents, we should also recognize the economic value generated through our encounters with non-humans (Haraway 2007).

we have non-human workers currently zipping along the aisles of Amazon warehouses moving bins of merchandise. Additionally "co-bots" (collaborative robots) are employed in manufacturing, working next to their human counterparts. So, work, broadly conceived, includes more than human agents. Nevertheless, we will restrict our discussion to human workers, leaving open the possibility that, in the future, examination of these debates may well need to include non-human workers.

From Peasant Class to Working Class

While work pre-dates capitalism, the way work is organized within a capitalist economy bears close scrutiny. It should come as no surprise that for capitalism to exist and sustain itself there must be a group of individuals who are able to labor. There also needs to be another set of individuals who employ workers in their business. While we take it for granted that there is a market for labor, with workers supplying their labor and employers demanding to hire workers, originally this relationship needed to be created. In other words, the labor market emerged out of the changing nature of economic and social relations that marked the transition from a feudal economy to a capitalist industrial economy. This transformation did not happen overnight. It took centuries, culminating in the fifteenth century when a multiplicity of factors undermined the feudal social and economic structure.[1]

Debates about what actually motivated the transition from feudalism to capitalism point variously to: (1) the rise of trade and the need for markets to facilitate the exchange of goods, and with it the need to clearly establish the rights to property; (2) differential agricultural productivity between farmers (serfs and free laborers) that allowed for specialization and the use of wage labor; (3) the shifting balance of power between lords and serfs and the changing nature of control over forced labor and free labor.[2]

The key relationship we want to explore involves the power of landlords (lords) and peasant farmers (serfs). The feudal economy was a system of agricultural production in exchange for physical and political protection. In brief, serfs were provided plots of land to raise crops to meet their families' needs after paying the lord his rent in the form of agricultural products. If a serf was especially productive and harvested more food than they required, they could sell their surplus crops in the market. However, in return for the use of the land and the physical protection afforded by the lord and his knights, a serf was required to toil in the lord's fields in order to provide food for the lord and the rest of the residents of the manor. This arrangement was held in place by the political institutions of monarchy and Church which granted property rights to the lords. Not only could peasants produce a surplus but the labor time that they devoted to tilling and harvesting the lord's land can be understood as surplus labor – labor over and above what is required to meet the physical needs of the serf. So there was an incentive for serfs to increase their own productivity when working for themselves but not when working for the lord (Brenner 1977, 42; Resnick and Wolff 1979, 14).

Serfs were essentially coerced to work for the lord. If they resisted, they could be denied access to the land, raising the threat of starvation. Some serfs did escape to the city. Others were able to buy their freedom with earnings retained from the sale of their surplus produce. So, over time, a variety of rent payments could be made: labor-rents, in-kind rent (agricultural produce) and money-rent. This is an important point to remember. The feudal system co-existed with markets, trade and proto-industrial production. In other words, there were a variety of economic activities beyond the lord–serf relationship that supported the feudal economy. Later on, we will find that a plurality of economic relationships and work practices also characterize the capitalist economy.

Notice that participants in the feudal economy using rent paid in the form of labor time and agricultural products started to interact with markets and money. Marx notes that, by the fifteenth century, most English serfs had become peasants working for a wage and free laborers leasing small land parcels. Market exchange did not bring about the development of a capitalist labor market. Rather, shifts in the balance of power between lords, serfs and the emerging classes of artisans and small manufacturers posed challenges to the dominance of the old system. However, the incipient manufacturing sector could not grow without access to ready supplies of workers. Here then is an important sub-plot to the story of the rise of capitalism. For capitalism to take hold, there was a need to transform peasant farmers into industrial laborers. This is a process that has been replayed across many countries over the last 500-plus years.

What it required was a segment of the population that lacked any independent access to the land and tools. Serfs were able to till their individual plots of land and provide subsistence to themselves and their family. Individuals without access to land and the means to produce what they needed to subsist had to sell their labor in the market in return for a wage. The wage was then used to purchase goods and services upon which the family subsisted. In sixteenth- and seventeenth-century Britain, lords began to consolidate small parcels of land in order to specialize in crop and livestock (e.g. sheep) production. This had the effect of dispossessing serfs and small tenant farmers, often transforming them into wage laborers (Brenner 1977, 78; McNally 1990). Capitalist forms of agricultural production were predicated on production for the market rather than for direct use by the producers. Furthermore, during the eighteenth and nineteenth centuries, a series of Enclosure Acts was passed by Parliament that expanded the lords' ability to take over and enclose land that was used in common by small farming families. Previously, grazing livestock on common land provided an economic buffer to families in which men hired out as agricultural laborers. Women participated in the household economy by utilizing these common lands (Humphries 1990; Neeson 2000). Between 1750 and 1850, over 4,000 separate Acts of Enclosure were passed by Parliament (Lazonick 1974, 26). The Enclosure movement was a long-drawn-out battle to transform communal land into private property. It, in itself, did not create the working class, but it did remove an alternative source of livelihood, thereby making families more dependent on the capitalist labor market for their very survival. As wage laborers cut off from the land, the former peasants could not fall back on farming to cushion the blow from wage cuts or unemployment. So, from the sixteenth through the nineteenth century, large segments of the British population came to find themselves with nothing to sell but their own labor as members of the new working class in the market-based economy (Polanyi 1944).

However, the capitalist labor market does not function like an automatic machine that adjusts labor demand to absorb the new members of the working class. The excess supply of labor created a cadre of unemployed workers reduced to begging in the streets. Throughout the sixteenth century, these vagabonds were criminalized and brutalized. Marx describes the penalties meted out to the unemployed under the reign of Henry VIII, including:

> whipping and imprisonment for sturdy vagabonds. They are to be tied to the cart-tail and whipped until the blood streams from their bodies, then to swear an oath to go back to their birthplace or to where they have lived the last three years and to "put themselves to labour" ... For the second arrest for vagabondage the whipping is to be repeated and half the ear sliced off; but for the third relapse the offender is to be executed as a hardened criminal and enemy of the common weal. (1887/2015, 522)

Being without work not only deprived individuals of the means to survive, it also was seen as an affront to the emerging system of capitalist production: "Thus were the agricultural people, first forcibly expropriated from the soil, driven from their homes, turned into vagabonds, and then whipped, branded, tortured by laws grotesquely terrible, into the discipline necessary for the wage system" (Marx 1887/2015, 523). From these harsh conditions arose the modern capitalist labor market and the world of work.

The capitalist wage system in the eighteenth and nineteenth centuries became the dominant force structuring not only the production of goods and services but also the composition of families, the character of leisure time and the overall quality of life, including life expectancy. Between 1550 and 1800, an average individual in Britain could expect to live to the ripe age of 37 (Clark 2007, 92). However, in the decades of the 1850s and 1860s in cities undergoing the most rapid industrialization, Manchester and Liverpool, the average life expectancy was around 30 years (Szreter and Mooney 1998, 88). In the United States during this period, a slave system of production co-existed with capitalism, and examples of slave, coerced labor are still found today (see Text box 1.2).

Text box 1.2 The interweaving of slavery and capitalism: cotton and seafood

Slave labor is by its very nature unfree and coerced. The labor market under capitalism is one in which workers are free to sell or withhold their labor from the market. One might assume that slave labor and wage labor are part of different economic systems. Indeed, this is the mainstream economic perspective. The mainstream view argues that the slave economy was a remnant of the pre-industrial, pre-market era and, as such, retarded economic growth. But, as we saw in the account of the transition from feudalism to capitalism, two systems of production can co-exist over long periods of time. Furthermore, in the case of slavery, particularly the nineteenth-century US slave economy, historians and political economists are beginning to identify ways in which slavery was embedded within a larger global network centering on the production and distribution of cotton (Beckert 2015).

Southern plantation owners borrowed money from banks, sold their cotton to merchants who re-sold it to textile mills, and purchased clothing, farm implements and other inputs from northern manufacturers. The slave worker was bought and sold in slave auction markets. They had no choice about who purchased them and what type of work they would do. But the amount of work performed – the number of pounds of cotton picked, for example – was something that the master had to extract from the slave. So this part of the work relation is similar to the relationship between worker and manager in a typical factory. Since the technology used in cotton harvesting was fairly simple and innovations were few and far between, the primary means of increasing output was to increase the pace of work. As a result, a brutal regimen of beatings was applied to the slave labor force. Sometimes, even the most productive workers were subject to severe, violent beating in order to generate a higher standard of output for everyone else to meet. As historian Edward Baptist describes it, "This is how clever entrepreneurs extorted new efficiencies that they themselves could not imagine. They pressed their most skillful hands and contriving minds even harder" (2014, 168). This is not to say that the capitalist market economy required slavery in order to prosper and succeed in the United States. Rather, it is to point out the way different forms of labor and work relations can co-exist, and indeed complement one another.[3]

Contemporary evidence of the relationship between capitalism and forced or slave labor practices can be found in the international fishing industry and, in particular, the unlicensed or pirate fishing vessels in Thailand and Indonesia. Ironically, it is the push of global competition leading to overfishing that compels fishing operators to search for the lowest-cost labor. That often means recruiting vulnerable migrant workers from Myanmar, Cambodia and Laos. Labor brokers find workers in these countries and, for a fee to be paid later, send them to employers in Thailand. That fee becomes a debt that binds them to work for the fishing operator. In addition, upon employment, they are told that they will be charged "runaway insurance" if they flee. According to one study of Thai fishing vessels, "Crew members can be subjected to substandard living conditions, including the lack of basic necessities such as drinking water, food, clean bedding and hygienic facilities. Long working hours are common, with extreme shifts being reported;

Continued

Text box 1.2 *(Continued)*

and commonly fishers are only permitted short breaks of 3–4 h[ours]" (Chantavanich, Laodumrongchai and Stringer 2016, 2). Yet these "pirate" fishing operators occupy a necessary link in the fish supply chain: "According to Eurostat, the UK has the largest appetite for Thai fish, consuming over €153.4m of it a year, closely followed by Italy, Germany, France and the Netherlands. Much of that will have been caught by pirates" (Neslen 2015). So slave labor, wage labor and the fish on your plate are part of the same system. Consumer awareness of the exploitative working conditions used to supply the fish market can help to bring about change to this system (Marschke and Vandergeest 2016).

Fast-forward to today and the world of work is a very diverse place, reflecting differences in scale (local–regional–national–global) as well as variations in the social and political environment in which work is performed. Nevertheless, there are some shared characteristics and patterns of work across the globe. For example, fewer and fewer workers perform paid labor in agriculture, while employment in manufacturing is stagnating. Instead, a growing number of workers from Germany to the UK and from China to India are working in the service sector and this trend continues into the twenty-first century (Table 1.1). Manufacturing is by no means extinct, however. In 2017, the proportion of the paid workforce employed in German and Japanese manufacturing resembled that of China. And across the globe men are disproportionately represented in manufacturing jobs. At the other end of the employment spectrum, in Sweden, the UK and the United States, approximately 4 in 5 workers and 9 out of 10 females are employed in the service sector. Services comprise a diverse array of jobs ranging from food service workers and caregivers for the elderly to professional financiers and computer information specialists. Looking at the data in Table 1.1 we can also find cross-national differences, notably the relatively equal proportion of men and women in the Chinese service sector. And in India men have a higher share of employment in services than women whereas women are disproportionately employed in agriculture, although the share is falling.

Table 1.1 Employment share by sector and gender, world and selected countries, 2000–2017

		AGRICULTURE			MANUFACTURING			SERVICES		
		2000	2017	Change	2000	2017	Change	2000	2017	Change
World	Total	39%	26%	−13%	22%	22%	0%	39%	51%	12%
	Male	38%	26%	−12%	24%	27%	3%	38%	47%	9%
	Female	41%	27%	−14%	19%	15%	−4%	41%	57%	16%
France	Total	4%	3%	−1%	26%	20%	−6%	70%	77%	7%
	Male	5%	4%	−1%	36%	30%	−6%	59%	66%	7%
	Female	3%	2%	−1%	14%	9%	−5%	83%	89%	6%
Germany	Total	3%	1%	−2%	34%	27%	−7%	64%	71%	7%
	Male	3%	2%	−1%	45%	39%	−6%	52%	59%	7%
	Female	2%	1%	−1%	18%	14%	−4%	80%	85%	5%
Italy	Total	5%	4%	−1%	32%	26%	−6%	63%	70%	7%
	Male	6%	5%	−1%	38%	36%	−2%	56%	59%	3%
	Female	4%	3%	−1%	21%	13%	−8%	75%	84%	9%
Japan	Total	5%	3%	−2%	31%	26%	−5%	63%	71%	8%
	Male	5%	4%	−1%	38%	34%	−4%	57%	62%	5%
	Female	6%	3%	−3%	22%	15%	−7%	73%	82%	9%
Sweden	Total	2%	2%	0%	25%	18%	−7%	73%	80%	7%
	Male	3%	3%	0%	37%	28%	−9%	60%	69%	9%
	Female	1%	1%	0%	11%	7%	−4%	87%	92%	5%
United Kingdom	Total	2%	1%	−1%	25%	18%	−7%	73%	81%	8%
	Male	2%	2%	0%	36%	28%	−8%	62%	71%	9%
	Female	1%	1%	0%	12%	8%	−4%	87%	92%	5%
United States	Total	2%	2%	0%	23%	19%	−4%	75%	79%	4%
	Male	3%	2%	−1%	33%	28%	−5%	65%	70%	5%
	Female	1%	1%	0%	12%	8%	−4%	87%	91%	4%
China	Total	44%	18%	−26%	28%	27%	−1%	28%	56%	28%
	Male	41%	15%	−26%	26%	31%	5%	33%	54%	21%
	Female	47%	20%	−27%	30%	22%	−8%	22%	58%	36%
India	Total	60%	43%	−17%	16%	24%	8%	24%	33%	9%
	Male	54%	38%	−16%	18%	26%	8%	28%	36%	8%
	Female	74%	56%	−18%	12%	18%	6%	14%	26%	12%

[*Note*: Reported differences reflect rounding up fractional values]
Source: International Labour Organization (ILO), World Employment and Social Outlook: Trends, ILO modeled estimates: www.ilo.org/wesodata.

While illustrative of recent shifts in the type of work people perform as paid laborers, this table does not describe all of the work that is done in the economy. Individuals who perform unpaid labor in families, or volunteer in churches, schools and their community, are not counted as working. But they are working, often accomplishing very difficult, productive and meaningful tasks. Other individuals not in the labor force may be disabled or unable to work for other reasons. Nevertheless, the category of people "not in the labor force" gives us a rough and ready measure of unpaid labor together with those who have been excluded from the world of paid labor (Table 1.2). Examining the data in Table 1.2 we see that in

Table 1.2 Percentage of working-age population *not* in the labor force (neither formally employed nor unemployed), selected countries, 1990–2017

		1990	2000	2017	Change 1990–2017	Change 2000–2017
France	Total	44%	45%	45%	1%	0%
	Male	34%	37%	40%	6%	3%
	Female	54%	51%	49%	–4%	–2%
Germany	Total	42%	42%	40%	–2%	–2%
	Male	28%	32%	34%	6%	2%
	Female	55%	51%	45%	–10%	–6%
Italy	Total	50%	52%	51%	2%	–1%
	Male	33%	39%	42%	9%	3%
	Female	65%	65%	61%	–4%	–4%
Japan	Total	37%	37%	40%	3%	2%
	Male	23%	23%	30%	7%	6%
	Female	50%	51%	50%	0%	–1%
Sweden	Total	33%	38%	36%	4%	–2%
	Male	28%	34%	33%	5%	–1%
	Female	37%	42%	39%	2%	–3%
United Kingdom	Total	37%	39%	38%	0%	–1%
	Male	26%	30%	32%	6%	2%
	Female	48%	47%	43%	–5%	–3%
United States	Total	35%	34%	38%	4%	5%
	Male	25%	26%	32%	7%	6%
	Female	44%	41%	44%	1%	3%
China	Total	21%	23%	31%	10%	8%
	Male	15%	17%	24%	9%	7%
	Female	27%	29%	39%	12%	10%
India	Total	39%	41%	46%	7%	5%
	Male	16%	17%	21%	6%	4%
	Female	65%	66%	73%	8%	7%

Source: International Labour Organization (ILO), World Employment and Social Outlook: Trends, ILO modeled estimates: www.ilo.org/wesodata.

2017 the percentage of the working-age population that is not in the labor force ranged from a low of 31 (China) to a high of 51 (Italy). While, with the notable exceptions of China and India, women have been more likely than men to be outside the paid labor force over the period 1990–2017, women have also been moving into the labor force. The situation for men is very different. Here the trend across countries is for more men to exit the labor force. Approximately 40 percent of working-age men in Italy and France find themselves outside of the formal, paid labor market. Even for those individuals who are in the labor force and have jobs, there has been a slow but persistent increase in the number of workers who are part-time. Currently, in Germany, Japan, Great Britain and the United States, about 1 in 5 workers are part-time (working fewer than 30–35 hours per week).[4] This illustrates the need to be open about recognizing work performed by those individuals who may not fit the stereotype we have of who a worker is.

National trends and patterns of employment are important, but it is also necessary to explore the structure and organization of particular workplaces and practices. While there are general trends that span regions throughout the world, notably fewer jobs in agriculture, negative or shrinking job growth in manufacturing and positive growth in service-sector jobs, there are also significant differences that need to be explored. One of the goals of this book is to highlight the diversity of workplaces and worker experiences within a capitalist economy. So, throughout the book, data will be presented that are specific to the issue being discussed.

The Unique Characteristics of Labor

The capitalist production process is predicated on the purchase of commodities, including land and machines, and labor[5] in order to deploy them in production and sell the finished product at a profit. Unlike in the feudal system, the purpose of capitalist production is not to satisfy the needs of the lord's manor, spend lavishly on luxuries or outfit more knights for battle. Instead, the goal is to produce a product that can be sold for money in the market. In Marx's terminology, the process extends from producing products solely for personal use (use value). The capitalist needs to produce goods that are useful to others, who are then willing to pay for them. They are valuable in exchange and therefore have exchange value. Marx went one important step beyond this and identified labor as the source of exchange value. So, in traditional Marxist political economy, the worker is the primary source of value, profit and economic growth. More generally, political economy, especially when compared to traditional, mainstream, neoclassical economics, understands that labor plays a unique role in the production process.

A second contribution to political economy comes from interpretations and extensions of the writings of John Maynard Keynes in the twentieth century. While Marx's ideas were shaped by his experience living through the industrial revolution, Keynes' worldview was deeply affected by the Great Depression of the 1930s. For Keynes, the question was whether capitalism, on its own, could generate enough work for all members of society. So Keynes looked at work in terms of the wage paid and the demand for goods and services resulting from workers' spending. Wages, along with business investment spending, constituted what Keynes called effective demand. The Post-Keynesian approach, while accepting Keynes' view of the importance of effective demand, also pays attention to the way in which work relations have been regularized through labor laws, union contracts and workplace regulations. In the Post-Keynesian world of work, individual worker decisions are always embedded within larger social and political regimes (Arestis 1996). For example, consider the dramatic decline in the percentage of workers who belong to unions. In 1954, 35 percent of US workers belonged to a union, compared with less than 11 percent in 2016 (Mayer 2004, 12; Hirsch and Macpherson n.d.). In Britain, the unionization rate was 52 percent in 1981, only to fall to less than half that figure by 2014 (OECD). The accompanying decline in the use of collective bargaining – where workers are represented by a union that negotiates with employers – has had a big impact on the balance of power between workers and employers in wage-setting. For both Keynesians and Post-Keynesians, capitalism is seen as incapable of generating enough jobs for all who want to work. As a result, the government has a role to play as an employer of last resort (Minsky 1986).

The common thread connecting Marxists and Post-Keynesians is the understanding that, through careful examination of the way work is performed, we can best explain the workings of the economy. So why is work accorded such a special place in political economy? We will describe four characteristics of labor that distinguish it from other resources used to produce goods and services.

First, unlike machines, factories and land, labor is inseparable from its seller. The owner of labor is the very same worker whose ability to work is bought and sold in the market and then employed in the production process. From this, it follows that workers retain control over the expenditure of labor effort. This makes the management of labor distinctly different from the management and direction of capital inputs (e.g. machines). Unlike with a machine, the capitalist employer cannot merely turn a knob to increase the speed of a worker. Directives to work faster may not be obeyed. As a result, control over labor is often conflict-laden. So, control, resistance and power are key dimensions of the workplace. Also, because labor is inseparable from the worker who sells it there are competing interests at work over wages. From the vantage point of a business owner, wages represent a cost of production, yet from the perspective of the worker wages are the money needed to buy consumer goods and services. This leads to a problem that has generated much disagreement among economists. Generally, mainstream economists have focused on the business perspective, so for them low wages are the key to higher profits and greater economic growth. Political economists, adopting a more worker-centered view, see wage-cutting as a recipe for disaster because the wage represents a source of demand for goods and services. Cutting wages is tantamount to cutting demand, thereby sinking the economy.

Furthermore, because labor is embodied in the worker who sells it, the skills associated with labor are also matters of conflict. Who decides what skilled labor is? This is a key concern today, given the growing number of low-wage workers and the increasing gap between low- and high-paid workers. Are low-wage workers necessarily low-skilled? Do highly compensated workers have truly exceptional skills? Skills, in the political economy view, are the product of social norms and values, including biases that result in the devaluation of women's caring labor and those jobs often performed by people of color.

Second, compared with other "inputs" into the production of goods and services, workers are produced not in factories but in families and schools. Workers' capabilities are developed within sets of social relations that exist outside of the workplace. Families are where we hope to get our basic needs – e.g. food, shelter, emotional support – met. Schools are where we develop socially and cognitively. As such, the necessary pre-conditions for a productive workforce involve the caring labor of parents, child care workers and teachers. Care work is carried out in families and in public – and, increasingly, private – educational institutions. Much care work often takes the form of unpaid or low-wage labor.

A third important distinction between labor and other resources used in the capitalist production process is that labor cannot be stored or turned off without losing its value. Unlike a machine or land, a worker who is unemployed for even a day is unable to recoup the lost earnings or lost productivity. A machine can be switched off for a day or a week without much maintenance to keep it in working order. Land taken out of production may actually increase its fertility, which is why crop rotation is a common agricultural practice. On the other hand, without work, there is no income, and without income, workers are hard pressed to purchase the necessities of life that will allow them to get a job tomorrow. Marx, commenting sardonically about freedom under capitalism, noted that workers are doubly free. They are free to sell their labor to the highest bidder, but they are also free from finding any employer willing to hire them. That is why unemployment carries such a heavy burden for workers by shifting the balance of power in favor of employers. With unemployed workers queuing up for your job, you might think twice about asking for a raise or complaining about your working conditions.

Finally, unlike with other inputs into the production process, the lived experience of work can influence our attitudes, values, norms and expectations regarding the meaning of work and the desire to work hard or to slack off. Behavioral economists study the motivation of individuals and the reasons why they act like they do. They note that both internal (intrinsic) and external (extrinsic) rewards are important in motivating workers to perform their best (Ariely, Kamenica and Prelec 2008). Money alone is not always enough to generate quality service. For example, child care work is among the lowest-paid occupations. Traditional, mainstream economists would be likely to predict that low wages translate into low skills with low levels of commitment to the children under care. However, there are numerous examples of caring, concerned workers willing to devote their time and energy to children in spite of the low wages (Folbre and Nelson 2000). This does not mean that low pay is acceptable, nor does it mean that child care work is low-skilled. What it means is that there are a range of factors involved in the organization of work that affect our desire to work hard or not. The political economy of work pays more attention to the ways in which our values depend on the structure of work.

These four characteristics that make labor unique in the production process are explained in more detail throughout the rest of the chapters of this book. In Chapter 2 ("Inequality at Work"), the issue of skills, wages and inequality will be the focus of our discussion. Traditional mainstream economics states that skills are acquired by individual workers. The more skills you acquire, the more valuable your labor is and the higher your wage. But is skill acquisition equally available to all? Furthermore, with the increasing prevalence of service jobs in which "people skills" are important, are these skills valued in the same way as technical or cognitive skills? Finally, is skill the only, or even the major, determinant of differences in income? These are questions that we will begin to answer using insights from debates in political economy.

Because labor is produced and reproduced outside of the workplace, there are a whole set of productive activities that consist of largely unpaid labor. In Chapter 3 ("Gender at Work: Caring Labor"), we will explore the importance of this kind of work within the context of the political economy debates over the economic impact of household labor and care work. Feminist political economy arose in the twentieth century as a criticism of both mainstream and political economics for their neglect of the productive work involved in child care, education, family nutrition and health care. The shift in care work from the household into the market will also be examined, especially in light of social movements calling for the payment of a living wage for workers involved in caring for the well-being of the young, the old and the infirm.

The idea that labor is inseparable from the worker is further explored in Chapter 4 ("Managerial Strategies: Low Road vs. High Road and Off-Road"). The focus of this chapter is on the range of strategies that managers use to elicit more work from workers in order to increase labor productivity and the surplus that workers create for their employers. Two primary methods have been deployed throughout most of the twentieth and twenty-first centuries. The first involves the use of discipline, penalties, threat of dismissal and the maintenance of division and discord between workers. This strategy represents the low road. The emphasis is on keeping wages low while keeping the threat of job loss high. These authoritarian practices are put in place in modern corporations in order to maintain profits. The alternative to the low-road is, not surprisingly, a high-road strategy. This managerial method uses high wages and good working conditions to encourage workers to work hard and stay loyal to the company. This strategy also uses the implicit threat of unemployment to motivate workers to work hard. The political economy approach toward understanding work argues that unemployment is a structural requirement of a well-functioning capitalist economy. This again raises the issue of a power imbalance. In order for the capitalist market economy to function, some people – currently around 13.7 million in the United States and 3.4 million individuals in the United Kingdom[6] – need to be unemployed or underemployed. Finally, in addition to the low road and the high road, there is an emerging type of employment relationship that can be called "off-road." This is best captured by the rise of the gig economy in which individuals piece together a work life consisting of several part-time jobs – for example, ride-share driver, web designer, furniture assembler. The question is are these liberating new forms of work or are they the advent of a new class of economically marginal, precarious workers – the precariat?

An alternative way of organizing work – worker cooperatives – is the topic of Chapter 5 ("Beyond Managerial Strategies: Worker Cooperatives"). In worker cooperatives, principles of democratic governance are used to re-design the decision-making process. Everything from personnel matters to investment decisions is determined by the workers themselves. Several case studies of worker-managed firms will be presented in order to highlight the diversity of firm size, industry and national context within which worker cooperatives exist alongside of, and in competition with, more traditionally managed firms. Beyond the scale of the individual firm, there are cooperative work relations that link firms within a region. The Mondragon cooperatives in Spain are the leading example. The economic performance of cooperatives will also be investigated in order to assess the claim that the governance structure of cooperative enterprises positively affects the motivation and commitment of workers. Debates in political economy question whether cooperatives are viable within a competitive capitalist environment. Additionally, we will explore discussion and debates surrounding the compatibility between cooperatives and the emergent solidarity economy.

The role of technological change and its impact on skills and the structure of jobs is the focus of Chapter 6 ("Technology, Automation and Skills: Restructuring the Workplace"). In this chapter, we explore how changing technology is restructuring the workplace. There is much disagreement among political economists about the effect of automation, artificial intelligence and machine learning on jobs. For instance, some political economists agree with the mainstream view that technical change is inevitable and necessary for economic growth and prosperity. There will be some workers hurt by new technology – namely, those workers whose jobs are no longer necessary: telephone operators, travel agents and filing clerks, for example. But the expectation is that new technology will be adopted because it is cheaper and more efficient and, over time, workers displaced by new technology will find jobs in a growing economy. Then there are political economists who feel that this historical moment is different. The very nature of technological change has changed. No longer is the story one of new machines being used to replace nasty, repetitive jobs. Instead, computer algorithms are designed to act on new information which allows machines to make more accurate and dispassionate decisions than a human worker. The threat of massive labor dislocation and the economic and social pain that comes with it is what troubles these political economists. We will examine whether technological change is different this time, and what impact it has on the future of work. Along the way, we will explore what an economy without work would look like. Proposals to de-link income from work will be discussed, and debates surrounding the future of work will be explored in the final chapter ("Conclusion: Future Worlds of Work").

2
Inequality at Work: Skills, Wages and Productivity

Income Inequality: The Rich and the Rest of Us

It is no exaggeration to say that growing income inequality is a, if not the, major problem of capitalist economies across the globe. It is a problem that has mobilized millions to take to the streets in protest. The political consequences of wage stagnation, unemployment and growing income inequality have threatened the neoliberal status quo. For example, resistance to neoliberal, global, free-market economic policies became a rallying cry for the Occupy movement across the globe and the Fight for $15 campaign in the United States. And yet it also brought forth nationalist movements in the US, Britain and Europe that, despite little evidence to back them up, blame immigrants for causing wage stagnation and lowering living standards (Shierholz 2010; Ottaviano and Peri 2012; Preston 2017). Their anger appears to be misdirected. As a recent Oxfam report argues, income inequality is a growing global problem, because

> All over the world we find that workers have been getting a smaller slice of the pie, while the owners of capital have been prospering. Even in China, a country where wages roughly tripled over the last

decade, total income, fuelled by high returns to capital, increased even faster. An increasing capital share is almost exclusively a bounty enjoyed by people at the top of the distribution, as the richest disproportionately hold capital. (Hardoon 2017, 12)

It is safe to say that income inequality has become the flash-point for political and social unrest around the world. While there is agreement in the streets and in the halls of government that large and growing income disparities are a threat to economic and social stability, economists disagree about the reasons for persistent and growing inequality between the rich and everyone else.

First, we need to recognize that not all income comes in the form of wages paid to workers who produce goods and services. Income can also be received from the rents collected from owning land or the returns to owners of capital and financial assets. When we look at wage income, beginning in 1980 and continuing to the present, the US has witnessed a growing gap between the highest paid wage-earners and everyone else. Even within the richest 10 percent of the US population, the bulk of income growth has gone to the richest 1 percent, especially the richest 0.01 percent. This can largely be accounted for by the growth of top executive compensation in large US corporations (Piketty and Saez 2014, 482). By contrast, wage inequality in Europe has stayed roughly constant. For example, in France throughout the twentieth and into the twenty-first centuries, the top 10 percent of wage earners received about 25 percent of total wages generated, whereas the poorest half of the French workforce has received between 25 and 30 percent (Piketty 2014, 272). Compare this to the US where the top 10 percent increased their share from less than 35 percent in the 1970s to nearly 50 percent in the 2000s. That means that 90 percent of US workers must divide the remaining 50 percent of wage income between them (Piketty 2014, 291). The spectacular rise in incomes of the top 1 percent of the income distribution since the 1980s is a phenomenon apparent in the US, Britain, Canada and, to a lesser extent, Australia (Piketty 2014, 316). Yet wage stagnation – slow or no growth in wages for the vast number of workers – is a problem throughout the developed world (Goodman and Soble 2017).

Critical Analysis: Human Capital Theory

For many mainstream, neoclassical economists, the income inequality story is a simple one. Your income is the direct result of your productivity, which depends, in turn, on your skills. So mainstream economists attribute wage inequality to skill inequality. But what are skills and where do they come from? That is a question that flummoxed economists throughout the 1940s and 1950s. Surprising as it may seem today, most economists up to that time classified schooling as leisure. Education was just one of many ways to spend one's free time away from work. For them, education was one good to purchase among the many others offered for sale (Schultz 1959). As a result of this conceptualization, while economists were busily measuring the quantity of goods and services produced, they were puzzled by the "extra" output that failed to be accounted for by either increases in machinery (capital) or increases in labor (workers or hours worked). Economists were literally unable to explain the determinants of about 50 percent of the economic growth in the postwar economy. They attributed half of the growth to increases in capital and labor, while the remainder – called the residual – was mysteriously labeled "total factor productivity." As economist Richard Nelson sarcastically noted, "A growth theory that explains half of growth and much of the variation in growth by an unexplained residual (which is, after all, what 'growth of total factor productivity' really is) is not much of a theory" (1964, 580).

It is important to put this theoretical shortcoming into historical context. During the period in which economists were struggling to explain economic growth, Cold War animosity between the US and the Soviet Union was gathering steam. In fact, economists frequently cited Soviet economic growth statistics as an implicit benchmark against which to measure capitalism's productive capacity (Fabricant 1959; Schultz 1959; Domar 1962). As a result, resolving the weaknesses of standard economic analysis took on more urgency. It is within this context that what became known as "human capital" theory was developed. The ascendancy of human capital theory corresponded to the military threat posed by the Soviets as a result of the successful launch of the Sputnik I and II satellites in 1957. This launch exposed the need for the US to quickly catch up to their Soviet counterparts in the fields of science, engineering and math. So, the human capital idea – that individuals rationally decide to invest in themselves to upgrade their knowledge and skills – had a swift and powerful impact on economic policy. As Holden and Biddle argue,

> Before 1958, "human capital" was little more than a suggestive phrase in economics, and played no role in discussions of education policy. Within five years, there was an active theoretical and empirical research program in economics organized around the idea that certain activities could best be understood as investments in human capital. Over the same short period, the new idea of public spending on education as a form of investment with a demonstrably high rate of return and the capacity to contribute to the achievement of important national goals was enthusiastically communicated to the public by opinion leaders, policy makers, and even a President. (2017, 569)

Some 60 years later, human capital theory continues to be the leading explanation not only of economic growth but also of income disparity and economic inequality. So, to understand political economy debates over income inequality, it is important to review the neoclassical theory of human capital against which political economy provides alternative explanations.

There are three interconnected parts of the human capital story. First is the idea that the old models of productivity growth only took into account the quantity of labor (workers and hours) and failed to recognize the importance of labor quality, represented by workers with more cognitive aptitude, skill and training (Schultz 1961, 1962). A second element of the human capital story is contained in the strong empirical relationship between lifetime earnings and years of schooling (Mincer 1958). Finally, the third piece of the human capital story involves re-casting the narrative as one in which the protagonist or hero of the story is the rational individual seeking to maximize their lifetime earnings by investing in additional years of schooling or training (Becker 1962).

So the main actor in the human capital account is the rational, self-interested individual with well-ordered preferences: I know what I want, I prefer this to that, and will therefore make decisions that are best for me. What makes this story novel is a plot twist that involves the transformation of the main character from an everyday worker/consumer toiling away in some retail or factory job into an investor seeking to maximize the rate of return on their asset. And they are the asset. The investment decision is straightforward. First, the assumption is that education and training improve the value or quality of one's asset (labor). In other words, more education or training enhances our skills. Furthermore, human capital theory assumes that the more skills that one acquires, the more valuable one is and the higher one's income should be:

$$\text{Education/Training} \uparrow \rightarrow \text{Skills} \uparrow \rightarrow \text{Income} \uparrow$$

An obvious question is: why not just acquire the maximum amount of education possible? The mainstream answer is that there are trade-offs, since time spent in school is time that could have been spent working, earning a living now. So some individuals may decide to continue working because the benefit of additional education is outweighed by the earnings lost by being in school. Schooling or training is costly when tuition, books, supplies and fees are included. But what if everyone had the same access to education because of government subsidies or need-based financial aid? Would that permit everyone to choose their preferred, income-maximizing, level of schooling?[1] Yes, say mainstream economists, but this does not mean that everyone will choose the same level of schooling. In the above diagram, the link from education/training to skills depends on an individual's innate ability. In other words, some individuals are better able to make use of an additional year of schooling than others. So, as savvy investors, high-ability people will invest more in education than will low-ability individuals. If education leads to higher income, then high-ability individuals will have higher income than those with low ability – first, because they are better able to translate education into skills; and, second, because they will, as a consequence, invest more in education. According to the mainstream view this helps to explain the problem of income inequality, which is really not a problem after all. More educated people are more able – or mainstream economists say that they are more productive – and therefore they reap higher income in return for their decision to invest in their human capital. In summarizing his theory of human capital, Becker states that,

> The general theory has a wide variety of applications. It helps to explain such diverse phenomena as interpersonal ... differences in earnings, the shape of the age–earnings profiles – the relation between age and earnings – and the effect of specialization on skill. For example, because observed earnings are gross of the return on human capital, some persons earn more than others simply because they invest more in themselves. Because "abler" persons tend to invest more than others, the distribution of earnings would be very unequal and skewed even if "ability" were symmetrically and not too unequally distributed. (1962, 48–9)

This last sentence was meant to address a long-standing puzzle that held that the distribution of ability in a given population was far less unequal than the distribution of income. Becker's answer is that, since abler people tend to invest more in education and training than less able persons, their rate of return on investment, and hence their income, will be even greater than initial differences in ability. This then leads to the conclusion that income inequality is largely due to differences in human capital investment and innate ability. So those who earn more are richer due to their own rational decision-making and their own superior ability. The poor, by contrast, are also rational decision-makers, who choose not to pursue an additional year of schooling because it would not appreciably increase their lifetime earnings. This decision may be the result of their inability to make productive use of the additional education. This, of course, begs the question of how innate ability is measured. Often mainstream economists identify income as a measure of ability, skill and productivity. But if we have been keeping track of the story, this is a very curious assertion. Differences in human capital are assumed to generate differences in skill and productivity, which are then used to explain differences in income. It is not unusual for mainstream economists to select income – what we want to explain – as a stand-in or proxy for education, skill or productivity. As MIT economist David Autor argues, "Although economists would typically view the wages paid to a job as the best summary measure of the job's skill requirements, lay readers may take some assurance that wages as a skill measure are highly correlated with logical alternatives, such as education and experience" (2010, 37). However, the fact that two variables are highly correlated is no substitute for understanding the nature of the relationship. So we are left with an unsatisfactory answer about the identification and measurement of skills and abilities.

In addition to these problems, while there are some components of ability that we can measure – cognitive aptitude and experience on the job, for example – there are many that we cannot: so-called "soft" skills such as people skills and personal character traits. So, like with the economic growth model of the 1950s, in mainstream models of income inequality, after all of the measurable skills are included, whatever cannot be explained – the residual – is attributed to "unobserved personal characteristics." At best, we are left to speculate about which characteristics might help us to better understand differences in income between individuals, and, by extension, income inequality throughout the economy.

Despite these drawbacks, human capital theory has come to dominate explanations of income inequality and poverty. Since economics is inherently ideological, it is not surprising that human capital theory is consistent with a meritocratic view of income distribution in which those who earn more do so on the basis of their own talents and skills. This view, in turn, supports the status quo which preserves the existing structure of class-, race- and gender-based power. This is also evidenced by the frequent exhortation that a more educated workforce is the answer to economic problems.

Since the discovery of human capital in the 1960s, much attention has been paid to improving the quality of labor. But what has not changed is the focus on productivity difference as the source of income inequality. By setting income as equal to productivity, mainstream economists rely on the theory of marginal productivity. This theory describes a world in which a worker's incremental addition to the value of the product or service that they produce determines their wage. In essence, it holds that wages received, from the lowest-paid janitor to the highest-paid chief executive, should reflect the productive contribution of each worker to the product they produce. We will see that this theory is at odds with the political economy explanations of income distribution. But what is important to note here is that the line of reasoning flows from productivity to income. Add human capital and we return to the diagram above in which more human capital generates higher productivity that in turn is rewarded by a larger wage income.

Political Economy Critiques of Human Capital Theory

In political economy, discussions and debates about wages, skills and inequality form a counter-narrative to the dominance of the human capital story. The key components of the political economy response include:

1   a critique of the link between education and skill
2   an explanation of the ways in which skills are defined and contested over time
3   a critical analysis of the connection between productivity and income
4   alternative explanations for the persistence in income inequality.

Education and skill

First, beginning with the publication of *Schooling in Capitalist America* (Bowles and Gintis 1976), political economists offered a direct criticism of human capital theory. In doing so, they also provided an alternative explanation of wage determination and income inequality. This research argued that, while there was a linkage between education and earnings, cognitive skill acquisition was not the reason. In other words, schools provided students with something other than cognitive skills that allowed the more highly educated to earn more money. Furthermore, differences in the level of schooling itself did not provide much explanation for differences in income.

Schools, it is argued, are social institutions that reflect, and act to reproduce, the existing class hierarchy. In other words, schools are mechanisms that develop the social and behavioral aptitudes consistent with an individual's location in the class hierarchy. So, students from white-collar or upper-middle-class families acquire skills relevant for white-collar, managerial occupations. Similarly, students from working-class, blue-collar families are provided with a course of study and social skills important for success in manufacturing jobs, and students from the poorest families receive the training and skills appropriate for entry-level service-sector jobs. Furthermore, family background tends to play a larger role in determining individual income than does education (Bowles, Gintis and Osborne 2008). What does this mean? It means that the mainstream assumption that schooling generates cognitive skills is tenuous at best. Certainly, research seems to support a link between cognitive skills (measured by test scores) and income. And there is also a measured link between education and income. However, there is weak evidence that schooling is the source of cognitive achievement. Furthermore, both schooling and cognitive skills explain less than half of the differences in income between the rich and the poor (Osborne 2008).

In response to these shortcomings of human capital theory, political economists propose an alternative framing of the issues. First, the ability to obtain an educational credential – a degree – varies by race and gender as a result of discrimination, social norms and stereotypes. For example, the "male breadwinner" model of family provisioning continues to dominate in many cultures and countries, whereby the man is designated the head of the family and therefore expected to provide for the economic survival of the family unit (World Bank 2011, 194–6). As a result, the allocation of educational opportunities corresponds to the prevailing patriarchal norms that privilege male participation in the labor market. When confronted with evidence that earnings differ between men and women with the exact same level of schooling, early proponents of human capital theory explained the difference in terms of the choices made by women to major in subjects

– teaching, for example – that complemented their innate superiority over men in the care and nurturance of children in the household (Becker 1981; Polachek 1981). Therefore, women were acting rationally to maximize the return to their investment in human capital. Even if we accept the somewhat dubious assumption that women are naturally better at nurturing and raising children, this begs the question of whether women would wish instead to develop skills and competencies in addition to those in which they supposedly already had an advantage. An alternative explanation from a political economy perspective is that women's career choices are limited due to occupational segregation structured by a gender division of labor. A policy goal of many feminist economists is to challenge these patriarchal gender norms by increasing female access to education, including active participation in creating and evaluating the curriculum, thereby promoting economic empowerment (Kabeer 2005). Economic mobility is also constrained (or enhanced) by one's race. Even after accounting for parents' education, there is a substantial portion of the difference in economic outcomes between blacks and whites in the US that is largely a factor of race (Hertz 2008). Furthermore, labor market discrimination is a very real phenomenon. Studies using job resumés of individuals identical in all respects save race find that people of color are far less likely to be offered a job interview (see Text box 2.1).

Text box 2.1 Does my name make me less employable?

The problem of income inequality must be understood in terms of the race and gender of workers in the economy. Both racial and gender discrimination compound the problem of inequality when people with the same education and skills receive lower income largely because of their race (non-white) or gender (female) or the intersection of race and gender (Latina). Discrimination can take place at several stages in the hiring process. In one study, for example, researchers created resumés: two high-qualification (high education, experience, honors, specific skills and knowledge of software programs) and two lower-qualification (lower education, little or no experience, no honors and no specific skills). Four names were also selected to be representative of race: two white-sounding names and two black-sounding names. The researchers surveyed people in Chicago and Boston to test the correspondence between the names and assumed race of the person with that name. Pairs of white/black names were then randomly assigned to the pairs of high-/low-qualification resumés sent in response to actual job ads placed by 1,300 employers in Boston and Chicago. The research question was whether race would influence the rate at which white applicants with the same-quality resumé as black applicants would be called back for an interview. The researchers discovered that white applicants (resumés) received a call back 50 percent more often than did black applicants. Furthermore, when factoring in the type of resumé, white applicants with a high-qualification resumé are more likely to get called back than white applicants with a lower-qualification resumé. However, there was no similar advantage for high-qualification black applicants. They were no more likely to get called for an interview than blacks with a low-qualification resumé. So employers seem to value the experience, skills, education and honors of applicants when a white name is at the top of the resumé, but when that same resumé is headed by a black name, these identical qualifications are less valued. On the basis of these results, the researchers state that there is no mainstream model that can explain these findings. Another study using a similar methodology focused on low-wage jobs in New York City. The finding there, too, was that blacks were less likely to get called back. In fact, "black and Latino applicants with clean backgrounds fared no better than a white applicant just released from prison. The magnitude of these racial disparities provides vivid evidence of the continuing significance of race in contemporary low-wage labor markets. There is a racial hierarchy among young men favoring whites, then Latinos, and finally blacks as the candidates of last resort" (Pager, Bonikowski and Western 2009, 792–3).

The political economy approach would explain these findings by arguing that race is an important category used to create and maintain difference and divisions in the workforce. One historical example of this is the hiring of blacks to take the place of striking white workers. This both created racial divisions between white and black workers and also allowed the factories to continue to operate and make profits for the owner (Gordon, Edwards and Reich 1982). So, as these studies illustrate, the preferential hiring of whites helps to maintain white privilege and white economic opportunities in the wider economy.

Second, the fact is that individuals are born and raised in families and often inherit the economic status of the family into which they were born. It has been estimated that about 20 percent of the economic status of individuals is due to the economic status of parents, even after accounting for parental education, wealth and the genetic inheritance of cognitive skills (Bowles, Gintis and Osborne 2001b).

The family is where workers are produced and reproduced, replete with their unique personality traits, values and sense of efficacy and personal identity. So, looked at from this wider angle, worker productivity is directly influenced by family dynamics and related patterns of socialization in neighborhoods and social and cultural institutions such as schools and churches/temples/mosques.

Whose work is skilled?

Evidence indicates that non-cognitive factors – social skills, attitudes, personality traits – are more important than education at explaining income inequality (Osborne 2008). But these non-cognitive skills and behavioral traits are rewarded differently in different occupations and industries. For example, in occupations for which assisting and caring for others is an important part of the job, it is male-dominated occupations (e.g. psychiatrists, firefighters) that receive higher wages and not female-dominated occupations (Pietrykowski 2017b). In this sense, the skilled performance of caring for and assisting other people is valued differently if performed in male or female occupations. So we can begin to understand that skills, as contributions to the production process, can be acknowledged and rewarded or ignored and discounted. This makes the definition and economic value of skills something that can be seen as contested and subject to the balance of power between workers, and between workers and employers.

For example, in early twentieth-century Britain, running textile machines was considered skilled work when men did it but unskilled work when women were operating the machines (Phillips and Taylor 1980). The history of the twentieth-century labor movement is full of stories of craft workers struggling to protect their skills in the face of technological change. For example, skilled metal workers were needed to shape and design the molds used to create metal parts but their jobs were being deskilled by the introduction of automated machine-making machines (Heron 1980; Hounshell 1984). Not only were skills threatened, but so too was the masculine identity of the workers themselves (Lewchuk 1993), since skill is always bound up with issues of race, gender and place.

Today, the service sector is the source of employment for most workers around the world. Is interactive service-sector labor – greeting and serving customers, fielding complaints and managing emotions – skilled or unskilled work? A study of two workplaces in modern China offers some surprising insights. In spite of the image of China as the world's factory, the majority of workers in China work in the service sector. Less than a third of the Chinese workforce is employed in manufacturing industries (see Table 1.1). The first case study looks at workers at a luxury hotel. Men were assigned jobs associated with manual labor in hotel security, luggage handling and banquet set-up. Women were given jobs requiring social interaction in the restaurant and at the hotel front desk. Having been accustomed by their parents to a political regime that sought to erase differences in the outward appearance of men and women, female workers needed to be trained to talk directly but deferentially, make eye contact and, most importantly, to carry their bodies in a way that conveyed elegance and refinement. Yet this training was not acknowledged as skill acquisition. Instead, it was characterized as a means to activate innate, if latent, femininity. As evidence of their invisibility, social interactive skills were not even listed in the job evaluation form managers used to assess employee performance (Otis and Wu 2018). Consequently, female hotel workers were classified as unskilled, whereas the males were skilled. Yet the same type of interactive social skills involving customer service, this time in a retail store, were defined as skilled work. Here the dividing line between skilled and unskilled work was mediated by whether the worker was urban or rural. Urban workers wielded more power in the labor market since certain jobs were off-limits to rural migrants to the city. Instead of gender, place of origin became the means by which skill was assigned. In China, discriminatory employment practices were reinforced by urban residents' feelings of superiority over rural migrants: "By casting their rural colleagues as deficient of civility, skills, hygiene, and intellect, urban workers highlighted the scarcity and therefore the value of their own abilities, thus forming the basis of a claim to possess a skill" (Otis and Wu 2018, 14). Rural workers were responsible for cooking all the meals in the store's restaurant yet their work was classified as manual and unskilled. Another important feature of the division of labor in the retail store was that the majority of rural employees were men. So it was not uncommon for the rural workers to ridicule the lack of physical strength and stamina of the female customer service workers. In this way, they sought to leverage their masculinity as a means to gain the respect denied them as rural workers (Otis and Wu 2018).

Productivity and income

In addition to the critique of the link between education and income, the connection between productivity and income also needs to be re-evaluated. The mainstream theory of marginal productivity predicts that an individual's income should mirror their productivity. The direction of the relationship is clear: productivity → income. However, it is equally plausible to argue that wage income acts as an incentive to work hard. In other words, receiving a wage increase today makes the cost of losing your job greater today than it was yesterday. This acts as an incentive to work harder in order to keep your job. Now the relationship looks like this: income → productivity. This is an important shift in our way of thinking because, instead of believing that wages only reflect individual skill, ability and effort, we can envision how the wage can be used as part of a strategy to induce higher levels of labor intensity or effort. Notice that we now include a third factor among the components of productivity: effort. Recall that the human capital theorists maintained that a worker could increase their productivity by getting more training and education, and that those workers with more innate ability would be better able to leverage education and training into higher income. The political economy approach views productivity in a much more dynamic way. So, in addition to thinking of productivity in terms of the acquisition of discrete amounts of training/schooling, productivity can also vary in response to employer incentives to change the work effort put forth by workers (Bowles, Gintis and Osborne 2001a).

This is not to deny that aspects of marginal productivity theory can be useful. But it is often used to define wage inequality as a direct reflection of productivity differences, instead of placing this relationship into a broader social, political and economic context in which wages are mediated and modified by factors other than productivity, such as bargaining power (e.g. union representation), product market power (e.g. monopolies) or rent extraction by corporate executives (e.g. corporate bonuses unrelated to individual or company performance). On the other hand, some features of marginal productivity theory are more compatible with political economy. These include the idea that productivity tends to decline with additional hours worked, and beyond a certain point becomes negative. Students pulling an all-night study session can identify with this experience. At some point, additional hours of sleep deprivation produce negative results. It follows, therefore, that, after some point, reductions in hours spent studying/working may actually increase productivity. A New Zealand company recently experimented with a four-day working week, keeping worker pay at the previous five-day level. They found that stress was lower, morale was better and productivity was higher (Sperling 2018).

Political economy perspectives on income inequality

A distinctly political economy approach to understanding the persistence of income inequality is the structural approach provided by Marxist and institutionalist economists. In particular, the theory of labor market segmentation was developed in order to explain inequality as a structural feature of the capitalist economy. In other words, instead of explaining inequality as the result of the rational choices of individuals, Marxist political economists argue that inequality is the outcome of class-based conflict between workers and employers. They would not deny the importance of cognitive and non-cognitive skills, but the distribution of skills and rewards results in separate and distinct sets of occupations and work experiences for low-wage and high-wage workers. These distinct labor market segments mean that low-wage workers in the "secondary" labor market rarely if ever get the opportunity to improve or re-define their skills and move into high-wage jobs in the "primary" labor market segment. There is no real choice to invest in human capital since schools act to funnel students from low-wage families into jobs in retail, service or child care, where wages are low, job security is lacking, and prospects for promotion are slim. On the other hand, children from wealthy families generally find themselves prepared for careers in white-collar, high-wage, stable jobs with plenty of room for advancement. The labor market segmentation theory developed to include a middle-tier segment represented by middle-income families, whose children often went into manufacturing or clerical jobs with some opportunity for training and advancement, especially if the job was unionized. Race and gender also factor in to the allocation of workers to jobs. Workers of color and women were more likely to be found in the secondary segment, whereas whites and males were more heavily represented in the high-wage primary sector. The Marxist theory of labor market segmentation argues that the racial and gender divisions of labor also function to divide workers across occupations and income levels (Gordon, Edwards and Reich 1982).

So it is quite possible that the connection between education and income runs from family income to education. In addition, education may not directly provide individuals with skills, but may instead act to allocate workers to jobs where skills may be acquired. This explanation assumes that education is akin to a commodity bought and sold in the market since, as is the case in the US, school funding is tied to the local tax base and local property values. Therefore, wealthy communities can allocate more money to their local schools. What if, instead, education was treated as a universal right available to all, regardless of income or property values? This would sever the connection between family income and the level and type of education available, thereby disrupting the class-based division of labor that allocates workers to jobs in the occupational hierarchy.

Furthermore, income inequality is exacerbated when jobs in the secondary and primary sectors are growing while mid-tier manufacturing and clerical jobs are declining. Some economists have argued that the introduction of new technologies tends to hurt workers employed in middle-tier occupations requiring routine tasks, because those are most likely to be automated. On the other hand, those workers whose jobs are enhanced through the use of technology, like computers, are the beneficiaries of technological change. If these workers are already located in high-paying jobs, these trends will exacerbate income inequality (Levy and Murnane 2005). These divisions are also played out in the political arena when, increasingly, immigrant workers find jobs in the secondary sector while globalization and deindustrialization, together with declining rates of unionization, reduce the number of reasonably well-paid middle-tier jobs (Hudson 2007).

While non-cognitive behavior has been shown to have an impact on wages, the wage effects differ by gender and class. For example, antagonistic and disagreeable behavior is found to raise wages for men but not for women (Mueller and Plug 2006). In addition, individuals who possess a high degree of efficacy – meaning that they exude confidence about their own ability to change their situation – tend to receive higher wages, whereas people categorized as fatalistic – feeling that they have little or no control over outcomes – tend to receive lower wages (Osborne 2008). These behaviors are partly influenced by the economic conditions within which people live. So an individual who comes from a wealthy family, attended the best schools and is economically secure is more likely to possess a strong sense of efficacy. Likewise, someone who grows up in poverty, lives in a neighborhood with high rates of unemployment and lacks economic security may be more fatalistic. Individual behavior is conditioned by one's racial identity, in addition to gender and class. As the authors of the study on resumés and call backs (see Text box 2.1) state, "employers seem to pay less attention to or discount more the characteristics listed on the resumes with African-American-sounding names. Taken at face value, these results suggest that African-Americans may face relatively lower individual incentives to invest in higher skills" (Bertrand and Mullainathan 2004, 1002–3). The forces of race, class and gender overlap, intersect and overdetermine individual behavior, and political economists examine work, and wages, in relation to the race, gender and class standpoint of workers.

So far, we have examined political economy explanations of income inequality at the scale of individual workers or groups of workers. But there are large-scale, macro-level theories of income distribution that also need to be addressed. Here the focus is on the division of income between workers and the owners of capital. Beginning with the Marxist perspective, we see that labor is the source of value because it is the active deployment of human effort that creates a product or service that has more value than the resources used to produce it. For example, let us assume that we hire a plumber from a plumbing firm that dispatches a worker to your house to fix a leaky pipe. The plumber uses tools and expert knowledge to transform a leaky pipe into one that no longer leaks. Suppose the leaky pipe took one hour to repair and the repair bill is $85. The cost of the tools is minimal since they last a long time and only a fraction of the tools and the repair van are used up, but they do transfer their value to fixing the leaky pipe, which we can estimate as $5. The largest source of value is the time and effort of the plumber. So, if the plumber is paid $25 an hour[2] and $5-worth of materials are used for the repair, that leaves $50 for the owner of the company. This is the value over and above the value of labor used to make the repair. This is the surplus value. So the share of value going to labor and capital will vary depending on the wage of the worker and the ability of the capitalist owner to extract more effort from the worker. Marx proposed two possible scenarios in which this relationship between capital and labor would lead to economic crisis.[3]

First, the ability of the capitalist to make larger and larger profits depends on the sheer size and volume of production. As factories became larger, so too did the machinery used to mass-produce products. As such, labor, Marx predicted, would comprise a smaller and smaller share of each individual product. The ratio of machinery to workers would grow. Yet workers were the source of value. As a result, the value of each individual product would fall and so, too, would the rate of surplus value or profit. This falling rate of profit would disrupt the world of the capitalists who would then be forced to seek out new, unexploited sources of profit – opening up new markets around the globe, for instance. But the story of declining profitability would eventually repeat again and again until new sources of profit were exhausted.

A second potential for a crisis of capitalism enters through the need for capitalists to keep wages low. Since the wage reflects the cost of maintaining workers' lives, wages could be cut if the cost of those goods and services that workers need – consumer goods – was reduced. This could happen in several ways: (1) via technological improvements in the consumer goods sector that lowered the cost of these goods; (2) by reducing the acceptable standard of living of workers themselves; (3) by shifting some of the costs of maintaining the workforce onto the state, through food stamps, housing subsidies and the like. In this way, employers could lower the cost of labor and divert more surplus to themselves. This would have the effect of worsening income inequality. It could also have destabilizing effects on the economy through either mass social protests, declines in consumer spending or both. Crisis might then lead the working class to effectively resist the downward slide of wages and living standards, and potentially re-make the economy along non-capitalist, pro-worker principles.

Although Marx discussed countervailing tendencies which would allow for crisis avoidance, there remains a need to explain the temporal or cyclical nature of crisis and recovery (Dunn 2011). A contemporary Marxist explanation of crisis is provided by the Social Structure of Accumulation model, in which the conditions for capital accumulation and profitability are undermined, resulting in a search for new institutions, rules and norms upon which to re-establish profitability. For example, the combination of rising inequality, debt-financed consumer spending dependent on over-valued assets like housing, and the repeal of the restrictions on US banks allowing them to engage in aggressive, risky investment activity promoted profitability, temporarily postponing an economic crisis, while also creating the conditions for the subsequent economic collapse in 2008 (Kotz 2015).

Post-Keynesian political economists focus their attention on the effects of a wage squeeze on the demand for goods and services. According to Post-Keynesians, contemporary trends in income inequality are the result of both stagnant wages and a shift in capitalist investments toward financial instruments offering higher rates of profit than traditional investments in plant, equipment and technologies that produce tangible goods and services. In short, there is a marked trend toward increased financialization of investment, a focus on short-term returns on investment, and growing reliance on financial innovation as a source of profit (Minsky 1977; Zalewski and Whalen 2010). In addition, not all wage earners are the same. They can be separated into workers and managers. This is where we find much of the increase in income inequality since manager/supervisor earnings have far outstripped the wages of production workers (Mohoun 2006). So, we have three economic sectors – capitalists, managers/supervisors and workers – each seeking to garner a larger share of the pie for themselves (Palley 2014). In the Post-Keynesian explanation, workers' wages depend on their bargaining power, which in turn is determined by the strength of labor unions and the overall state of the economy. Strong unions are those that represent a sufficiently large proportion of the workforce to have an impact on the overall wage structure. Note that this does not require that a majority of the workforce be unionized. The threat of unionization is enough to compel employers of non-unionized workers to match the wage gains of their unionized competitors. As for the state of the economy, workers are able to gain better wages and benefits when unemployment is low and the economy is growing. So the balance of power shifts in favor of workers when unions are strong and the economy is at or near full employment. This led one economist to declare that full employment was incompatible with a capitalist economy since it shifted the balance of power away from capital and toward labor (Kalecki 1943).

Reflecting Keynes' interest in the demand side of the economy, Post-Keynesians understand wage inequality as a drag on economic growth (Carvalho and Rezai 2015). Since poorer people tend to consume more of their income, robust wage growth at the bottom of the income distribution would be more of a stimulus to total or aggregate demand. By contrast, savings are greater among the wealthy, but those savings may not necessarily be borrowed and used by investors. Investment decisions are dependent on the state of the economy, expected economic growth and potential profits (Kaldor 1955). In addition, the tendency for the capitalist system to enter a crisis of insufficient aggregate demand can be identified in the re-distribution of income not only from the poor to the wealthy but also through workers' increased reliance on consumer debt, and the resulting interest finance charges incurred in trying to maintain their standard of living (Onaran, Stockhammer and Grafl 2011).

Another perspective in political economy is offered up by institutionalist economics. The institutionalist approach focuses our attention on the particular structures, rules, habits and social norms or values that guide our behavior and govern our interactions with one another. From the institutionalist political economy perspective, one reason for the rising share of income going to the top 1 percent is found in the increased reliance on stock options and bonuses for chief executives, especially in the US. The rationale for using these payments can be linked to increasing incentives and changing social norms that make "rent-seeking" behavior acceptable. In rent-seeking, the rents are sums of money siphoned off due to some unearned advantage. The money comes from profits that could otherwise be re-invested in the company or paid out to shareholders of the company's stock. The argument here is that falling marginal tax rates (especially in the US) created an incentive for those at the top to channel more compensation their way. Over time, this became an accepted norm that weakened the links between executive pay and company performance (Bivens and Mishel 2013). Of course, an alternative use of this money would be to increase workers' take-home pay.

The problem of income inequality viewed through the lens of political economy highlights the interplay of power, class, gender and race played out in factories, shops, offices and homes. The analysis of income inequality reveals, but it also conceals. What is hidden is the unpaid work performed in making and maintaining a home, feeding and caring for children and the elderly, and building and sustaining one's community. It is to these issues of care work that we next turn our attention.

3
Gender at Work: Caring Labor

Identifying Care Work in the Economy

Is all work paid? Are skills rewarded differently in the labor market because of the gender of the individual applying those skills? Can the tasks that women traditionally perform in the household – for example, cooking, cleaning and child care – be analyzed as work? These questions lie at the heart of the research originally undertaken by feminist economists in the twentieth century.

The answer to the question "What counts as work?" is crucial to our understanding of various roles workers occupy in the economy, the products and services they produce, and the way in which employment practices and policies are structured and administered. Back in the mid twentieth century, the answer to the question was something upon which almost all economists and social scientists could agree. Work was identified with wage labor. Marxist economists took a more nuanced view of wage labor by distinguishing between productive labor – that which produced surplus value or profits for capitalists – and unproductive labor – work that that did not directly create surplus value. But they could agree that housework was not really work, since: (a) it was not exchanged in the labor market for a wage; or (b) it did not produce surplus value. Since most housework was, and still is, done by women in heterosexual couples, the fact that housework was not considered worthy of economic analysis reflects a bias against taking women's economic activity seriously.

Indeed, housework is not included in calculations of the national output of goods and services – Gross Domestic Product (GDP). Think for a moment about the peculiar consequence of excluding housework. If you buy a meal at a restaurant, the market value of that meal is included in GDP estimates. However, if you cook a meal at home, the value of the labor that goes into preparing the food and transforming raw materials (vegetables, spices, fish/meat) into a cooked meal is not included in GDP. So there is an enormous amount of work that is not included in estimates of economic activity (Waring 1990). If it were counted as part of a nation's output of goods and services, unpaid household labor would increase GDP by roughly one-third.

Who Performs Housework Around the Globe?

When we talk about housework, we mean the unpaid labor used to maintain a home and care for family members. This is why it is also referred to as unpaid care work. It involves tasks that contribute to what political economists call "social reproduction." Social reproduction refers to the fact that care is provided to develop and maintain the health and well-being of current (adult) and future (children) laborers. The political economy perspective, informed by feminist social theory, finds that in most societies gendered social norms have defined housework as women's work. Mainstream economics, informed by human capital theory, sees women as better suited to housework, given their large investment in child bearing. Yet evidence from heterosexual couples in which the father has extended time off from work to parent a newborn suggests that this gender division of labor is not biologically determined (Rehel 2014).

Responding to critiques by feminist economists, mainstream economists have begun to take more seriously the shortcomings of neglecting unpaid household labor or care work in their calculations of GDP. One estimate attempted to put a value on unpaid housework by using the wage of a professional housekeeper together with time use studies – daily logs of how individuals in families spent their time.[1] For the United States over the time period 1946–97, researchers found that including unpaid household labor resulted in a 43 percent GDP increase in 1946 and 24 percent increase in 1997 (Landefeld and McCulla 2000, 300). The reason for the smaller impact in 1997 can be largely explained by women's entry into the paid labor force. As a result, more market goods and services (e.g. laundry and day care services) were used in place of women's unpaid household labor. But even as more women worked full-time, men did not pick up the slack and do more housework. Instead, women work a "double shift," and the time spent on housework comes from time formerly used for leisure or sleep. Males and females without a paid job also allocate their time differently, with women doing substantially more housework and men engaging in more leisure activities such as watching television (Katz 2015), or performing more flexible household maintenance tasks that are not required for daily social reproduction (Moreno-Colom 2017, 18).

Large differences in the amount of time men and women spend doing unpaid caring labor is evident across the globe:

> The day-to-day lives of women around the world share one important characteristic: unpaid care work is seen as a female responsibility. Across all regions of the world, women spend on average between three and six hours on unpaid care activities, while men spend between half an hour and two hours. Hence gender inequalities in unpaid care work are observed all around the world, even if there are regional variations. Women devote an average of two to ten times more of their time than men on unpaid care activities. (Ferrant, Pesando and Nowacka 2014, 2)

Further data suggest that the male–female gap in household labor time is shrinking, with men doing some more work in the home. A 2014 cross-national comparison shows Sweden, Denmark and Norway with the most equal division of unpaid work between men and women, while Turkey, Portugal, Mexico and India are the most unequal, with women working well over 3 hours a day more than men (Figure 3.1). However, in the United States, Canada, Australia, Finland,

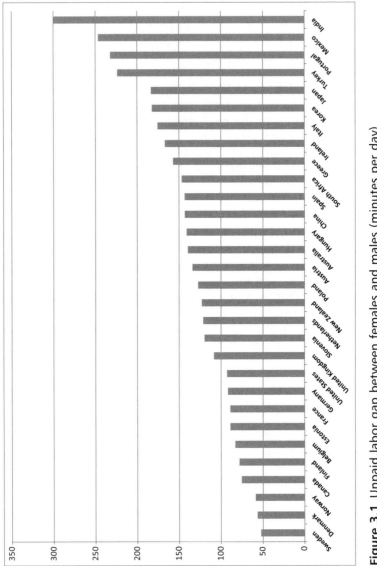

Figure 3.1 Unpaid labor gap between females and males (minutes per day)
Source: OECD (n.d.)

Netherlands, United Kingdom and Norway, the gap stopped shrinking and may have actually reversed itself (Altintas and Sullivan 2016, 464). The situation in China is similar to that in other parts of the world with urban women working an average of 10.5 hours per week more than men providing unpaid labor. In terms of support for working families, China, which has expanded the market-based sector of its economy, is reducing state support for child care, thereby shifting the burden onto the household sector or the private market (Dong and An 2015, 558).

Data from around the globe also indicate that men's unpaid labor increases as women enter the labor market (Ferrant, Pesando and Nowacka 2014). One explanation for this phenomenon is that, as women enter the paid labor market, they increase their economic bargaining power in relation to their spouse or partner. This explanation rests upon the bargaining model of household labor.

Bargaining and Power in the Household

The bargaining model assumes that individuals are self-interested and that their control over economic resources is the primary source of power in the household. Working in the labor market generates a key economic resource: income. Income earned in the labor market is a source of power not only because it allows the family to purchase necessities, but also because it provides the income-earner the option of leaving the relationship and setting up an independent household. By contrast, household labor is unpaid and, while it generates valuable goods and services for the family, it also leaves the partner who devotes more time to housework with fewer monetary resources to fall back upon in the event that the relationship dissolves. In addition, labor market discrimination and the devaluation of skills associated with women's work means that inequality in the labor market affects who does more (or less) housework. Note that this does not require that anyone perceives that housework is necessarily unpleasant or undesirable. Some aspects of housework, such as child care, baking and cooking, can be rewarding and fulfilling. Rather, the idea is that, since housework is not paid, it does not directly generate income and this reduces bargaining power.

Divorce or break-up is the ultimate threat in the family relationship. So the balance of power between partners in the household depends on: (a) their participation in paid labor or the ease of finding a job if they are currently not employed in paid work; (b) the wage that they could obtain in the labor market or the probability of finding a new partner earning an income at or above that of the current partner; (c) accumulated personal savings, and level of support offered by the state in the aftermath of divorce (e.g. family, job training and education support); (d) the strength of patriarchal social norms relative to principles/policies endorsing gender equality (Lundberg and Pollak 1996; Agarwal 1997).

The bargaining model of household labor further predicts that the time devoted to housework will become more equal as partners' income approaches parity. So, based on this theory, we would predict that, in cases where the roles are reversed in the labor market (women make more money than their male partner), roles should become reversed in the household (men should assume more household tasks and spend more time than their partner in unpaid housework). In dual-career couples who work outside of the home, researchers found that for every hour women spend in unpaid housework men spend only 35 minutes (Bartley, Blanton and Gilliard 2005, 97). In addition, women who earn more than their male partner should, according to bargaining models, have a superior fall-back position and therefore more power in the relationship. Actually, they end up performing more unpaid housework. One explanation for this unexpected outcome is that female partners compensate for transgressing the gendered norm that males should earn more than their female partner (Bittman, England, Sayer, Folbre and Matheson 2003).

It is worth noting that the representative family in bargaining explanations of housework is a stereotypical heterosexual married couple. But how does the division of household labor play out in same-sex households? Most of our insights about the division of labor in same-sex households come from qualitative studies using surveys, daily logs and interviews. The most common finding is that same-sex couples (gay and lesbian) contribute more equally to unpaid housework than do heterosexual couples. But this is not always the case, so we should not assume that same-sex couples have more egalitarian norms regarding who does the housework. An equally important issue arises from interviews in which respondents are asked about the meaning of both the division of labor between paid market work and unpaid housework, and the meaning of the particular household chores that are done by one partner or the other. In other words, do same-sex couples' perceptions of housework mirror the prevailing gender norms of heterosexuals that define housework as women's work? In cases where one partner spent more time in paid work and the other did more housework, lesbian couples understood that their situation could be perceived as reproducing male–female gender roles. Some couples were uncomfortable with that dichotomy and sought to resist it. The resistance came about, in part, by valuing housework equally to paid labor (Goldberg 2013). This was especially the case in one study of lesbian couples in Japan who felt that housework was a valuable and worthy endeavor that was best shared equitably (Kamano 2009). One take-away from this research is that lesbian and gay couples consciously attempt to re-define the gendered meanings of housework. For example, out of a set of ten routine household tasks, heterosexual, lesbian and gay couples were asked to identify whether the task was more feminine or masculine. The lesbian couples' classification was very different from the heterosexual couples' assignment of a task to a gender. Furthermore, in the case of gay couples, there was not even a clearly defined agreement on the gender-identification of most tasks (Goldberg 2013). What this indicates is that the gender norms associated with household tasks are more fluid and mutable than is usually assumed. It also informs us that the dominant heterosexual, male–female distinction is not the only way to think about the gender division of labor between unpaid housework and paid labor.

Finally, the assumption that children are always recipients of household labor and not active participants in their own right needs to be challenged. Children also perform household tasks. Again, there are distinct variations in the amount of time boys and girls spend on housework. According to one study of US families, girls spend 30 percent more time doing household chores than boys. In addition, boys are 15 percent more likely to receive an allowance than girls (University of Michigan 2007). This result is not specific to the United States, and has been found in Nepal where younger female siblings do more housework than their older brothers (Edmonds 2006). A study of 16 countries in Asia and Africa revealed that in 11 out of the 16, children worked more than 15 hours per week either in household labor or in a family-run business, with girls working mainly at home (Webbink, Smits and de Jong 2012, 640). However, other researchers have identified cultural differences in the way that children participate in household labor. In one study of Mexico City, comparing middle-class, educated families to poor indigenous families, there were stronger expectations of service to the community among children of indigenous families. By contrast, in middle-class families, household work was defined in terms of a limited number of specific tasks for which a child was individually responsible. The researchers explain that, "Emphasis on [middle-class] children's self-care and individual ownership of tasks based on personal belongings, spaces, and chores may help socialize children to commodity-focused relationships in which work and responsibility are tied to individuals and contract principles of economic exchange" (Coppens, Alcalá, Mejía-Arauz and Rogoff 2014, 126).

Care Work: Paid and Unpaid, Inside and Outside the Home

In addition to uncovering the hidden (in plain sight) economic contributions of women's household labor, feminist economists have called attention to caring labor. Caring labor involves the development and maintenance of individual well-being by providing social, emotional, cognitive and physical support services to others. In addition, caring labor, or care work, primarily involves face-to-face interaction (England, Budig and Folbre 2002, 455). Jobs such as teacher, nurse, therapist, social worker and the clergy are examples of care work occupations. Three dimensions of care work are especially useful to explore.

First, care work involves actions oriented to other people. It is intended to improve the life of at least one other person. As a result, the recipients of care work can better utilize their capacity for productive work, either now – for example, in the case of adults who successfully complete a literacy class at a community center – or in the future – take the example of children who receive asthma screening and treatment at a local health care clinic. In this sense, care work develops what political economists refer to as "capabilities" that enable people to obtain a high quality of life and a standard of living measured not in terms of income or possessions but in terms of what is socially and culturally appropriate to ensure personal well-being. Good health, adequate education and personal security are some of the foundations without which individuals cannot develop their own capabilities. But self-efficacy, mobility and political participation are also included in this list (Sen 1999; Robeyns 2003; Alkire 2005). Many of these prerequisites for the development of one's capabilities depend on having access to care workers who can provide fundamental services (education, health care, security). Note that the goal of enhancing capabilities is not to accelerate economic growth. The focus is on the individual and her or his ability to make a better life, a life which may or may not lead to economic growth. For example, suppose that you have a high-wage job that you do not like because it does not make use of your creativity, talent or passion. By developing your abilities, you might be able to achieve a better life for yourself while earning a lower wage that adds less value to the total economy. While capabilities theory focuses on the individual, individuals are embedded in social institutions, groups and communities. The capabilities approach begins to unravel the tight connection in mainstream economics – discussed in Chapter 2 – between individual choice regarding income and skill acquisition and its impact on economic growth. If we have access to teachers who can instill in us confidence, self-worth and an outlet for our creative talents, we can make choices that could lead us toward personal fulfillment and away from the highest-paying job and the most economically productive use of our time. This choice may loom especially large in capitalist economies that are prone to crises marked by unemployment, underemployment and wage stagnation.

The second feature of care work that sets it apart from other types of work is the social interaction inherent in the successful performance of care. More specifically, as feminist economists Folbre and Nelson (2000) point out, care work can, but need not, involve both caring for someone and caring about them:

> The word "care" has a dual meaning, on the one hand referring to caring activities, like changing diapers or providing a listening ear, and on the other hand to caring feelings, like those of concern or affection on the part of a caregiver. Caring feelings on the part of the caregiver are assumed to provide a motivation for doing caring activities, and to assure the effectiveness of the care received. Ideally a care recipient should feel authentically "cared for," nurtured, recognized and valued as an individual, emotionally supported, empathetically connected, or, in shorthand, loved. (129)

The recognition that care work involves a degree of what sociologists refer to as "emotional labor" is important. You would not expect your auto mechanic to personally care about you, let alone develop an emotional attachment to your car. But you would probably like to know that the child care worker who looks after your daughter cares about the well-being of your child and even develops a healthy concern about your child's emotional and cognitive development. The question arises whether paid care work decreases that level of commitment on the part of care workers. In other words, does the child care worker take a more instrumental view of her job, seeing the child as a means through which to secure a paycheck? Furthermore, does payment for a service decrease the quality of care, maintaining "caring for" but reducing the emotional commitment involved in "caring about" your child?

We can raise similar questions about many occupations in which a monetary payoff can warp one's concern for the well-being of others. The financial crisis of 2008 was rife with examples of financiers trading toxic assets (risky mortgage-backed securities) that ended up enriching them at the expense of individual homeowners and the overall economy. So this is not an argument that only applies to care work. However, the mainstream solutions to an undersupply of "caring about" reflect the gendered lens through which caring labor is understood. The solutions are to: (1) insist that care is best undertaken in the household by parents, which, as we have seen from time use data, means mothers much more than fathers; (2) pay a low enough wage so that care workers could not possibly be thought to take on these jobs just for the money. The first option rests on either the dubious assertion that mothers are more efficient at unpaid care work or the patriarchal claim that husbands should be primarily responsible for work in the paid labor market – the "male breadwinner" thesis. The second option assumes that people receive psychological benefit or intrinsic rewards from participating in paid care work, so their total benefit (monetary + psychological) is what matters. The lower wage compensates for the higher intrinsic reward, compared to a job without such benefits for which the wage would need to be higher. An alternative explanation is that, due to discrimination or lack of power, workers – notably workers of color and women – may not have a choice other than to take the job or be unemployed.

The discussion so far has focused on low-wage care work. But not all caring labor pays low wages. Health professions, for instance, include high-wage care jobs such as those of physicians and health care specialists. Since the 1980s, both high-wage care work occupations and low-wage caring occupations have grown. This growth at the high and low ends of the wage distribution helps to partly explain growing inequality in jobs and wages. Interestingly, jobs involving nurturing skills, such as those in child care, teaching and health care, best represent this bifurcated growth pattern. On the other hand, jobs that involve reproductive caring labor – cooking, cleaning – remain clustered at the low end of the wage distribution (Dwyer 2013).

Efforts by feminist economists and sociologists to better understand the economics of care work have focused on the economic return to care occupations. Since most – but not all – care work is performed by women, researchers try to disentangle the effects of gender on occupational wages after taking into account factors such as the industry in which the jobs are located, educational requirements, and demographic factors of employees in caring occupations – such as age, marital status and race. The results of empirical studies tend to show that there is a wage penalty for holding a job in a care work occupation (England 1992; Kilbourne, Farkas, Beron, Weir and England 1994). Even men suffer a wage penalty – lower wages than a similar individual employed in a different occupation – upon entering a caring occupation (England, Budig and Folbre 2002). The wage penalty for working in caring occupations is fairly consistent across countries (Budig and Misra 2010). Recent evidence suggests that even workers who do not directly provide caring labor but who work in a caring industry also suffer a wage penalty compared with workers with similar jobs in other industries (Folbre and Smith 2017).

Devaluation Thesis and Gender Bias

Men get paid more on average than women, and this is what is known as the gender gap in earnings between males and females. In the 1970s and 1980s, as more women moved from the household into the labor market, they took jobs in the small set of fields (teaching, nursing, food service and clerical professions) open to them. In the United States, this story pertains mainly to white women, since women of color had been employed earlier as domestic workers cooking and cleaning in private households, but also increasingly in offices and later in jobs that transferred domestic labor into laundries, cafeterias, hospitals and janitorial services (Glenn 1992; Duffy 2007; Alonso-Villar and Del Rio 2013). This resulted in a pattern of employment wherein women were segregated into a small number of occupations by gender, and also by race. A trend up until 1980 was for women of color to occupy jobs similar to those of white women. So, while racial segregation declined between white women and women of color, gender segregation between males and females persisted (Albelda 1986). As more and more women entered the labor force, the supply of workers in occupations deemed suitable for women also went up and wages went down. This is known as the crowding theory. However, even as women moved into more male-dominated occupations and occupational segregation declined, wages remained low so that the entrance of women into male occupations actually pushed down wages (England, Allison and Wu 2007). Furthermore, since 1980, the gap between white women and black women and Latinas has grown as white women moved into professional and managerial occupations (Alonso-Villar and Del Rio 2013).

Table 3.1 illustrates the stark racial differences between women's occupations. The data represent the distribution of majority female occupations by racial composition in the United States. For example, nearly 98 percent of speech-language pathologists are women, and whites make up 85 percent of this occupation. Similarly, 90 percent of licensed practical nurses are female, and blacks comprise over 30 percent. Over 90 percent of all housekeepers are women, and over 43 percent are Latina. These data reveal the sharp differences in occupations performed by white women and women of color. The average wage of these occupations also illustrates the greater representation of white women in professional jobs. Also note the prevalence of the titles "assistant" or "aide" among the black and Latina occupations. As sociologist Evelyn Nakano Glenn notes, "Whatever the setting, aide work continues to be a specialty of racial-ethnic women. The work is seen as unskilled and subordinate and thus appropriate to their qualifications and status" (Glenn 1992, 30).

One explanation that feminist economists and sociologists advance for occupational segregation and wage differentials between majority male and female jobs is that women's jobs are associated with feminine traits or skills that are less valued. This devaluation reflects cultural biases and social norms that shape our understanding that jobs have feminine or masculine characteristics. One way to understand this is to recognize that we[2] have a tendency to classify the world in terms of binary categories: objective/subjective, quantitative/qualitative, individual/social, male/female (Nelson 1998). These dual categories are read as opposites and, furthermore, these opposites tend to be associated with assessments like "favorable" or "unfavorable," "better" or "worse" (Nelson 1996). From a feminist perspective, the last in the list of pairs

Table 3.1 Top 10 US occupations for women, by race (2016)

White		Black		Latina	
Occupation	Median annual wage ($)	Occupation	Median annual wage ($)	Occupation	Median annual wage ($)
Speech-language pathologists	74,680	Licensed practical and licensed vocational nurses	44,090	Maids and housekeeping cleaners	21,820
Dental hygienists	72,910	Maids and housekeeping cleaners	21,820	Medical assistants	31,540
Nurse practitioners	100,910	Child care workers	21,170	Dental assistants	36,940
Medical records and health information technicians	38,040	Dietitians and nutritionists	58,920	Child care workers	21,170
Secretaries and administrative assistants	37,230	Teacher assistants	25,410	Personal care aides	21,920
Dietitians and nutritionists	58,920	Medical assistants	31,540	Receptionists and information clerks	27,920
Registered nurses	68,450	Billing and posting clerks	36,150	Tellers	27,260
Preschool and kindergarten teachers	34,010	Receptionists and information clerks	27,920	Teacher assistants	25,410
Payroll and timekeeping clerks	42,390	Preschool and kindergarten teachers	34,010	Health care support occupations	27,910
Hairdressers, hairstylists and cosmetologists	24,260	Hairdressers, hairstylists and cosmetologists	24,260	Office clerks, general	30,580
Average	**55,180**	**Average**	**32,529**	**Average**	**27,247**

Source: Occupation Employment Statistics (OES), May 2016, US Bureau of Labor Statistics; Current Population Survey 2016, US Bureau of Labor Statistics

mentioned above – male/female – works as an organizing principle whereby masculine traits are evaluated favorably whereas female traits are not. So not only is this a dualism but it is a hierarchical dualism with one of the pairs occupying a higher status than the other. As Nelson (1996) explains it, "The hierarchical nature of the dualism – the systematic devaluation of females and whatever is metaphorically understood as 'feminine' – is what I identify as sexism. Seen in this way sexism is a cultural and even a cognitive habit, not just an isolated personal trait" (7). For example, mainstream economists privilege objectivity over subjectivity, quantitative or mathematical research over qualitative analysis, and the individual over the social. This view of the world adopts the vantage point of the individual scientist examining the world objectively by collecting and analyzing quantitative data to test a mathematical model. Picture in your mind the scientist and you may probably imagine a man. This gender-bias influences the hiring process and the wage workers receive for doing work that is considered male or female. Let us look at one example of the impact of sexism on work in order to demonstrate this de/re-valuation process.

A common stereotype of computer software developers is of young men with top-notch analytical, technical and cognitive skills, but perhaps lacking in interpersonal and social skills. As one historian of computer technology put it, "Since technical skill conveys power – including prestige, access to well-paid employment and the opportunity to shape the tools used by a whole society – the dominant groups in society tend to assert their 'natural' superiority in these fields. In particular technical expertise has been an important component of masculine identity in Western culture" (Abbate 2012). In 2016 80 percent of all computer software developers in the United States were men. The question is: do males have an inherent superiority in software development? It is common to label analytical skills requiring math and science as "hard" skills, whereas interpersonal skills receive the moniker "soft" skills. In light of this hard/soft dualism, it should come as no surprise that in the 1950s and 1960s, the early days of the computer industry, it was *hard*ware development that was considered to be the more masculine pursuit. By contrast, *soft*ware was open to women and was considered an extension of the counting, filing and sorting tasks associated with clerical work. And clerical work was done by women. As one historian of computing explains:

> In the first textbook on computing published in the United States, for example, John von Neumann and Herman Goldstine outlined a clear division of labor in computing ... that clearly distinguished between the "head-work" of the (male) scientist, or "planner," and "hand-work" of the (largely female) "coder." In the Goldstine/von Neumann schema, the "planner" did the intellectual work of analysis, and the "coder" simply translated this work into a form that a computer could understand. "Coding" was a "static" process that could be performed by a low-level of clerical worker. (Ensmenger 2010, 123–4)

The reality of the situation was that coding and programming remained a highly skilled and lucrative source of employment open to women (Abbate 2012). Future control over the occupation depended on whether software development was going to itself be coded as masculine or feminine (Cohen 2016). The gendered character of software development was being contested in the 1960s and 1970s. The struggle involved a desire on the part of employers to recruit and hire the most productive employees. This involved a process of screening potential employees by giving them a battery of tests that were supposed to measure both the technical aptitude and the personality traits consistent with a successful programmer. However, the technical tests focused on mathematical prowess, even though math was not a predictor of success. In addition, the personality test for programmers tended to value individuals who preferred to work in isolation and who were generally anti-social and independent. Not surprisingly, the successful recruits tended to look more and more like the contemporary cohort of computer programmers and less like the women who were the first to perform the tasks of coding and programming (Ensmenger 2010). So, in this example, gender traits, skills and personality characteristics were used to select workers. The occupation of computer software developer was re-defined as software engineering and cast as a masculine pursuit, even though the relevant skill set did not change and women excelled in the job prior to the use of personality tests and subsequent re-definition of the gender norms associated with the occupation of software developer (Abbate 2012).

Another study, covering the period 1970–2007, finds that, as women entered high-paying male jobs, those jobs became more closely associated with female characteristics and wages subsequently declined (Mandel 2013). Furthermore, even as occupational segregation has fallen for women entering the professional fields in law, business and medicine, the route to upward mobility is more difficult for working-class women for whom few career ladders are available to move up and out of jobs in retail, clerical work, food service or child care (England 2010). Indeed, one needs to ask who is doing the work in the household when women devote more time to managerial and professional paid work. Often the work at home is performed by low-wage immigrant workers and women of color. Seen in this way, the gender binary – male/female – obscures an analysis of the ways in which hierarchies of work reflect class and racial divisions within gender categories. In other words, the experience of a female Jamaican child care worker and that of a female bank manager complicate the picture of caring labor. The debate over the distinction between caring labor, emotional labor and interactive social labor brings us back to the early debates over social reproduction and the work performed in the household and in the labor market to maintain a steady supply of labor.

Care Work and Social, Emotional Skills

The type of work necessary to maintain the labor force extends beyond the traditional categories of care work. In particular, personal service providers – such as hairdressers, manicurists, trainers – help to reproduce workers' physical appearance and sense of self-efficacy and self-confidence, to be sure. But hairdressers, along with food service workers such as bartenders, also provide emotional support through their ability to empathize with their clients and patrons. While, as we have seen, many care work occupations suffer a wage penalty, we can also identify a set of caring skills and investigate the economic return to specific skills. One study

(England 1992) found a negative return – a wage penalty – to nurturing skills. A more recent study of caring skills finds that the same skill has differential returns depending on the gender composition and the class position of the occupation. So low-wage occupations for which "assisting and caring skills" are important suffer a wage penalty, whereas high-wage occupations are rewarded with a wage premium. Men in high-wage occupations received a wage premium for caring skills and for "social perceptiveness." Women, on the other hand, receive no wage boost for social perceptiveness skills. Low-wage workers in general, and those in majority female occupations, did receive a wage premium for skills associated with "establishing and maintaining interpersonal relationships." Finally, low-wage workers in general earned a wage penalty for skills associated with service ("actively looking for ways to help people") (Pietrykowski 2017b). One explanation consistent with the devaluation thesis is that skills that are typed as "feminine" are not rewarded in the labor market because they are perceived to be innate, natural attributes of women (Guy and Newman 2004).

Much person-to-person service-sector labor involves the performance of emotional, as well as physical and cognitive, labor. Workers who perform emotional labor manage their own emotions in order to meet the expectations of both employers and customers. While there is overlap between care work and emotional labor, emotional labor expands the boundaries of our analysis of work and gender. For example, 86 percent of all US police officers are male, whereas 90 percent of all nurses are female. However, it was found that the jobs of police officers and nurses entail similar levels of emotional labor (Steinberg and Figart 1999).

The original study of emotional labor involved flight attendants whose job it was to display a range of emotions intended to keep customers feeling safe and comforted, and perhaps also distracted from the thought of rocketing through the air in an aluminum tube (Hochschild 1983). Additionally, they also try to manage the emotions of their customers. Flight attendants' interactions with passengers involve strategic, skillful and sometimes creative forms of emotion management. For example, one flight attendant reported her experience providing meal service to a hostile passenger who ended up flinging a cheeseburger at her face. She effectively managed his emotions and gained the support of the other passengers by suspending meal service to the entire flight until the passenger apologized to her over the plane's public address system (Bowe, Bowe and Streeter 2000, 161–3).

Providing service to others not only requires the management of emotions. It also demands bodies that are appropriate to the service or product being marketed. Recall from Chapter 1 that labor is unique among the inputs that are used to produce a good or a service. Labor effort – the capacity to work – is embodied in the person of the laborer. Therefore, managerial control over the production process extends to control over individual workers. This takes on an added dimension when we consider the case of interactive service workers. Since worker behavior is an essential part of the service, employers feel legitimately compelled to "intervene in workers' looks, words, feelings, thoughts, attitudes and demeanor, not only in the motions of their bodies and the uses of their time" (Leidner 1999, 84). In addition to emotional labor, work also entails the performance of what is known as aesthetic labor. Through aesthetic labor, employers can and do make use of workers' bodies – faces, hair styles, physiques, body modifications, voices – to enhance the economic value of the service being provided (Warhurst and Nickson 2007). Recent attention to the embodiment of work helps to extend the concept of emotional labor to managing one's physical appearance and personal style. Such embodiment can even occur in services that are not face-to-face, such as the way in which Indian call-center workers serving US clients try to erase any trace of an Indian accent in order to create an impression that the customer is talking to a fellow American (see Text box 3.1). Aesthetic labor also applies to interactive, face-to-face service work that makes use of the physical appearance of the worker as a part of the service transaction. Mainstream economists have recognized that there is a beauty bias in the labor market. People traditionally thought of as good-looking tend to receive higher wages than average- or below-average-looking individuals in the United States (Hamermesh and Biddle 1994) and Britain (Harper 2000). Adopting this mainstream logic, if rational employers were indifferent to their workers' appearance, they would

Text box 3.1 Emotional and aesthetic labor in the call center

Consider the case of a call-center technical support worker in India. Call centers employ approximately 700,000 workers in India alone (Locke 2017). These jobs are assumed to require few skills, where skills are narrowly defined along the dimensions of cognitive and physical aptitude. But when viewed from the vantage point of emotional and aesthetic labor, the picture changes. First, while Indian call-center workers are native English speakers, they need practice and training in order to speak an "Americanized" form of English, in order to effectively interact with US callers, many of whom claim to not understand them or are rude to them when they use their own Indian English (Mirchandani 2004, 360, 366). This is a form of aesthetic labor whereby the call-center worker needs to manipulate their voice, speech patterns and pronunciation in order to sound American. They must hew closely to a given script but also be able to adapt to the customer's level of familiarity with and technical knowledge of the product being supported, all the while keeping their emotions in check. For instance, emotion management is called upon when customers mistake a computer's CD drive for a cup holder (Mirchandani 2004, 362). Finally, the call-center workers must orient their lives with reference to the customer's clock, calendar and geography. Call center workers are adept at preparing to interact with the customers in the zone that they have been assigned. This means reading up on the news from the previous day. A 2003 study of call-center workers describes how a worker "knows the Bulls lost last night ... glances at the many clocks on the wall to see what the time is in Tulsa. In order to get a sense of how to put the whole package of American-ness together, he has been watching *Friends* and *Baywatch* in his training sessions" (Poster 2007, 272). An Indian call-center worker must work at night to synch to US business hours and be familiar with seasonal customs and holiday traditions in order to effectively carry on a conversation (Mirchandani 2004, 364; Poster 2007). In order to minimize racial animosity and racist customer reactions, both the worker's native speech and their location are hidden. But not all call-center workers are compliant with the demands to act and speak American. Some workers accommodate the demands of their employers in order to keep their job, but remain ethically opposed to the practice of assuming a fictive identity. Still others object to having to specifically portray an American (Poster 2007). So, through an examination of the emotional and aesthetic demands placed on call-center workers, we see that such work requires a repertoire of skillful self-presentation and politico-ethical practices that are not easily reducible to the traditional cognitive (brain) / physical (brawn) dichotomy.

refrain from hiring attractive workers in order to avoid paying them a wage premium. On the other hand, looking at the market from the political economy perspective, we see that the majority of occupations for which aesthetic labor is important are low-wage occupations in retail clothing, hospitality and food service (Warhurst and Nickson 2007). In addition, even within industries like retail clothing, aesthetics can often shade into racial and gender bias in the workplace (Williams and Connell 2010).

Household Labor and Social Reproduction: Past, Present and Future

What has also come under scrutiny by feminist historians, political economists and social theorists is the central – yet by no means necessary – role played by the traditionally defined household as a family unit. Household production and social reproduction can and do take place on a larger scale: take public schools as the more popular alternative to home schooling. Similarly, one can imagine a community of families who prepare meals, wash clothes and maintain property collectively, using community-owned resources. Indeed, we need not imagine such a community since the historical record points to many such housekeeping cooperatives and housing collectives across North America, Britain and Europe in the late nineteenth century. In the United States, feminists and socialists issued plans to change the very physical design of cities in order to break down the separation of private households from social life (Hayden 1981). Their goal was "to invent new forms of organization in the neighbourhoods that could make the hidden domestic work visible. The new interventions included housewives' cooperatives, new building types (kitchen-less houses; apartment hotels), day care centres, public kitchens, community dining clubs and food service delivery" (Vestbro and Horelli 2012).

For example, the Cambridge Cooperative Housekeeping Society began in 1870. It was a white, middle-class experiment that attempted to professionalize housekeeping services by employing workers – often workers of color – to perform tasks of social reproduction such as laundry service. Middle-class cooperative members were hired as supervisors to oversee the work of the laborers, who were paid wages higher than the going rate (Spencer-Wood 2004). Similarly, pioneering feminist economist Charlotte Perkins Gilman, in 1898, advocated for the construction of kitchenless apartments and homes:

> The apartments would be without kitchens; but there would be a kitchen belonging to the house from which meals could be served to the families in their rooms or in a common dining-room, as preferred. It would be a home where the cleaning was done by efficient workers, not hired separately by the families, but engaged by the manager of the establishment; and a roof-garden, day nursery, and kindergarten, under well-trained professional nurses and teachers, would insure proper care of the children. The demand for such provision is increasing daily, and must soon be met, not by a boarding-house or a lodging-house, a hotel, a restaurant, or any makeshift patching together of these; but by a permanent provision for the needs of women and children, of family privacy with collective advantage. (Gilman 1998, 242)

Notice that the idea is to centralize some of the most labor- and time-intensive aspects of caring labor necessary for social reproduction. Gilman explicitly mentioned professional women and families as those who would most benefit from this collective provision of care work. As in the Cambridge Cooperative before it, the labor involved in cooking and child care would be done by paid domestic workers. A few attempts were made to establish collective housing for domestic workers along with training programs leading to unionization, but they were ultimately unsuccessful (Hayden 1981, 171). So, while this model moves beyond the atomistic family unit and the gender division of labor within the family, it remains tied to a class and racial hierarchy in which some women and families are able to hire the labor of other women to do the work of caring and social reproduction (Glenn 2012).

More recently, feminists have begun to critically re-assess and re-visit past socialist and communitarian efforts to construct alternatives to family provisioning embodied in new models of collective housing in Denmark and Sweden. During the 1980s, approximately 40 collective housing programs were established, using a cooperative system of care work and social reproduction. In other words, instead of hiring workers to perform household labor, the residents themselves – men and women – shared in the responsibilities and tasks of cooking and cleaning for one another (Vestbro 1997). In Denmark, Copenhagen's Christiana neighborhood exists as commons in which private residential property ownership and alternative forms of communal social reproduction arrangements co-exist (Jarvis 2013). What these examples point to are potential post-capitalist forms of economic life. They are post-capitalist in the sense that they are predicated on meeting common needs and aspirations that are often at odds with the need to provide a productive labor force (Federici 2012). In that sense, they also challenge the Marxist viewpoint.[3]

The traditional Marxist idea is that relationships of hierarchy and power in the workplace are reproduced in the family. In the Marxist feminist literature, the capitalist employer benefits from the unpaid labor of housewives by allowing wages to be kept below what they would need to be if all costs of social reproduction were incurred in the market. A radical approach would be to sever the connection between social reproduction and caring labor. In other words, the goal of social reproduction is to provide for the supply and maintenance of productive workers now and in the future. This conforms to the Marxist feminist view that the family unit is a capitalist-serving institution. But it need not be. In other words, as Maria Mies argues, "A feminist concept of labour has to be oriented towards the *production of life* as the goal and not the production of *things and of wealth* of which the production of life is then a secondary derivative" (2014, 217). By production of life, Mies means the production of useful goods and services that benefit communities. This begins to cut the connection between work and profits – namely, that one works to earn a wage, and a wage is paid in return for working in a profit-making enterprise. Caring labor is important and necessary but it need not be either directly commercialized by hiring others to perform care work or tasked to individuals who lack the power to re-balance the gender division of labor. "Nobody, particularly no man, should be able to *buy* himself free from this work in the production of immediate life" (Mies 2014, 222). This perspective directly opposes not only the mainstream view that women are naturally suited to household labor but also the view held by some political economists that women's access to paid labor is the solution to gender inequality.

4

Managerial Strategies: Low Road vs. High Road and Off-Road

Major Themes Defining Work Under Capitalism

For most of the time and in most occupations, work is a social experience. Imagine a lonely writer toiling away in a cabin far in the woods. Even a reclusive writer needs to be in contact with an editor, meet deadlines and be productive. Even if authors bypass this route and self-publish, their work is exposed to social acclaim, criticism or indifference. And the audience's enthusiasm has an effect on book sales and, by extension, the writer's income. Even the most isolated work is embedded in the social organization of production. Marx referred to this as the social relations of production. In the transition from feudalism to capitalism, the object of production shifted from production for use to production for exchange. The goal of survival and family subsistence was replaced by that of profit-making through the generation of surplus value over and above what was needed to reproduce workers.

So now, in the modern capitalist economy, work becomes a means to an end because it entails working for someone else whose goals and aims are different from the goal of the individual worker. Now workers work in order to earn an income that can be used to buy goods and services. In the past, the feudal worker – the serf – worked part of the time to produce their own necessities and part of the time to produce goods for the lord. Nowadays, workers are employed in occupations that meet the needs of their employers by producing products and services that realize a profit but do not directly meet their own needs. The division of labor came about largely to allow employers to expand the scale of production by limiting the breadth of skills a worker needed to produce a product. For example, five workers each directed to complete one discrete task in the production process could produce more than fifteen workers who are each required to perform all five tasks by themselves. This division also ensured that workers would never be able to directly produce their own necessities.

This division of labor involved the subdivision of jobs into a larger number of smaller tasks. Adam Smith's example of the division of labor involved the fabrication of a simple pin. He identified 18 tasks that went into making a pin (Smith 1776). Each of those tasks could be assigned to an individual worker. Similarly, Henry Ford enumerated 11 specific tasks that went into making a metal spring (Ford 1926). These two production processes, separated by 150 years, contained the same basic principle: by breaking down the entire job into its specific components and hiring workers who specialized in one simple task, employers eliminated the need for skilled craft workers who knew each step of the process and how they fitted together. Adam Smith believed that this division of labor improved worker dexterity and, by extension, worker productivity. Focusing on a single task also permitted workers to devise innovations in the way their job was done. The knowledge of the entire production process and how the subdivided tasks fitted together was now entrusted to a new occupational group known as overseers or managers. Yet Smith was also aware of the negative effects the division of labor had on workers – namely, the experience of monotony and boredom that accompanies simple, repetitive tasks. Early manufacturers even referred to their workers as mere "hands" to be deployed alongside machines.

Marx used this experience of the division of labor in manufacturing as the basis for his concept of alienation. In his view, assigning workers to specific tasks allows for the scale of manufacturing employment to grow: "The habit of doing only one thing converts him into a never failing instrument, while his connexion with the whole mechanism compels him to work with the regularity of the parts of a machine" (Marx 1887/2015, 243). The goal was to make workers more like machines that could be more easily controlled. In addition, while a worker's dexterity is increased by focusing on one or two small steps in the whole production process, the division of labor under capitalism "converts the labourer into a crippled monstrosity, by forcing his detail dexterity at the expense of a world of productive capabilities and instincts" (Marx 1887/2015, 450). So workers' capacities, their ability to learn, to create and to envision the entire system of production – perhaps even conceptualizing a different, less hierarchical system – are stunted as they become alienated from the process of production. Alienated labor is alive and well today in the service sector. Consider the case of Grant Lindsley who worked for Google as a "talent channels specialist" – a person who invites prospective Google employees to apply for a job. Grant's job entailed using software to "customize" recruitment messages by including the individual's name and day of the week. Grant also conducted the initial interview, consisting of "10-minute phone calls with interested candidates, conversations comparable in depth and variation to a drive-through order at Burger King." If the interview was positive, another HR person took over. If the interview didn't go so well, Grant would send the candidate a standard (yet personalized) rejection message. This represents the extent of his job, repeated an average of 40 times a day. Grant reflects that "In some ways, my experience is not so different than that of other twenty-somethings in corporate America. Yet Google's low-level HR employees are barraged by higher-ups about Passion! and how we are Changing People's Lives!" (Lindsley 2017). The lack of meaning, disconnection from the job and overall lack of control over how the work is done are the hallmarks of alienated labor (Shantz, Alfes and Truss 2014).

The capitalist division of labor involves a separation between those who work and those who oversee the work process, or, in the words of twentieth-century labor scholar Harry Braverman, between execution and conception.

Braverman uncovered the roots of modern human resource management theory in early scientific experiments on the human element in production. Scientific management, also known as Taylorism – named for its promoter Frederick Winslow Taylor – involved the careful analysis of workers' physical movements as they went about their tasks. By streamlining a worker's movements to only those absolutely necessary to accomplish a task in the shortest amount of time, scientific management aimed to increase worker productivity by essentially making workers more like machines. In addition, the subdivision of work into smaller and simpler tasks meant that workers did not need to develop higher-order skills or gain knowledge through apprenticeship programs. In fact, workers who formerly possessed craftsmen's skills found themselves "deskilled" in jobs that no longer required knowledge of integrated tasks. And these less-skilled workers could be more easily replaced. The system of large-scale mass production was well suited to the division of labor by task, the simplification of tasks and the standardization of workplace skills. So the modern twentieth-century division of labor ushered in a set of social relations of production that shifted power away from workers and toward managers. It also allowed employers to pay these workers less (Braverman 1974; Spencer 2000). Although Braverman painted a rather bleak picture of capitalist control and worker subjugation through deskilling, it is only a partial account.

While the goal of capitalist employers may be to render workers completely subordinate to the will of their corporate masters, unlike machines workers can and do resist. Furthermore, the capitalist enterprise combines collective labor processes requiring workers to coordinate their actions with one another and with equipment aimed at producing a large and growing profit. This creates a set of tensions between workers and between workers and managers and employers. On the one hand, the removal of craft-based distinctions between workers in large production facilities like Ford's massive River Rouge factory, employing over 100,000 auto workers, facilitated the organization of workers into industrial unions. On the other hand, there are strategies that managers can use to discourage collective resistance and to persuade workers to compete with other workers and to identify with the company (Burawoy 1979; Edwards 1979). In addition, the deskilling process is not irreversible and has been replaced at times by the need to re-skill workers in order to implement new flexible, computer-aided technology.

For most workers toiling away in a capitalist firm, the structure of their work experience is shaped by the need for employers to turn a profit. The means to that end are, however, not straightforward. Recall that, since labor is a peculiar input into the production process, the goal of making a profit depends on getting workers to produce an ever-growing surplus over and above that which is necessary to sustain the workforce. We can identify two distinct strategies that employers may use to elicit more work from workers. Note that these are ideal types, meaning that in practice employers may modify, combine and switch strategies depending on factors such as national and global competition, union presence and trade-offs between short-term profitability and long-term sustainability. We can give a name to the two ideal strategies: low road and high road. This metaphor was coined by union leaders in the 1980s and subsequently adopted by economists (Kochan, Katz and McKersie 1986, xii).

Low-Road Workplace Strategies

When discussing the ways in which management structures work, we need to recognize the variety of strategies available. They include forms of work relations that we would not normally associate with the capitalist standard of free markets and freedom of choice. There is, for example, a lively debate among historians and economists over the degree to which slavery, when it co-existed with capitalism, came to adopt managerial strategies that closely resembled those used in capitalist enterprise. The brutal institution of slavery was organized by an overseer who, together with the plantation owner, managed the work of the slaves. While slavery pre-dates capitalism and shares many features in common with feudal labor – unfree workers toiling for the benefit of others under harsh conditions of direct control enforced through violence or the threat of starvation – the slave system of production continues to co-exist alongside capitalism. In fact, the methods used to calculate the productivity of slaves, tracking the precise number of bushels picked per day per slave, and the violence meted out for missing production targets mirrored later developments in scientific management (Rosenthal 2016). This is not to deny that additional motives which may have conflicted with profit-seeking were at work under slavery. Nor does it discount the contribution of other sources of improved productivity in the slave system (Clegg 2015). But it does highlight some of the similarities and continuities between capitalist and slave systems – both based on power, control and the extraction of surplus labor.

Strategies consistent with the low road have been a hallmark of capitalist management since the rise of the modern factory system. While some employers experimented with more benevolent approaches to the management of labor, the "drive system" was used extensively in the early years of the twentieth century. As economist Sumner Slichter commented in 1920:

> In order to create a docile and subservient attitude on the part of the men and cause them to submit readily to being driven, managements deliberately sought to foster fear of themselves among the men. To this end they maintained as a matter of policy a brusque, more or less harsh, distant and stern attitude toward their men. They resorted to discharge on fairly slight provocation. They discouraged the airing of grievances. The man with a complaint was told, "If you don't like things here, you can quit." (44)

The drive system sped up the pace of the assembly line in order to increase worker productivity, forcing workers to do more work in less time. This strategy worked well in periods when workers were in plentiful supply or when there were pools of potential recruits – for example, farm workers, black sharecroppers and immigrants – who were new to factory labor. In addition to creating and maintaining a despotic system of intimidation through arbitrary firings and harsh discipline, the drive system also sought to push labor costs down to their lowest possible level. This was effective if there were few viable alternatives to factory work, which is often the case during the initial phases of industrialization. And agricultural workers facing starvation when their crops failed, black sharecroppers barely able to survive under feudal conditions, and recent immigrants who lacked the resources to return home all lacked alternatives to working under the drive system.

Lest one thinks that the drive system is a vestige of the past, employers revert to using it when economic conditions allow (Kaufman 2001). Indeed, the practice is alive and well in factories that supply smart phones, e-readers and game consoles. For example, Slichter wrote this about the drive system in 1920: "The drive system recognizes no standard day's work. On the contrary the aim is constantly to force up the speed of work" (41). Compare this to a 2011 first-hand account of working conditions at a Chinese factory operated by Foxconn, one of the world's largest employers and an Apple sub-contractor:

> Foxconn has adopted a production model apparently based on classic Taylorism. The production process is simplified to an extreme degree so that workers need no specialised knowledge or training to perform most tasks. Technicians from the industrial engineering department regularly use stop watches and computerised engineering devices to test workers. If they are able to meet the quota, targets are increased to the maximum possible. On the iPhone assembly line, another worker described how her tasks were measured to precise seconds: "I take a motherboard from the line, scan the logo, put it in an anti-static bag, stick on a label and place it on the line. Each of these tasks takes two seconds. Every ten seconds I finish five tasks." (Chan 2013, 88)

Frontline workers' sitting or standing posture is monitored as much as the work itself: "I had to sit in a standardized way. Stools have to be in order, and cannot move past a yellow and black 'zebra line' on the floor" (Chan and Pun 2010, 7). Foxconn's industrial engineering strives to make all workers' operations, up to the minutest movements, ever more rationalized, planned and measured. Each assembly-line worker specializes in one specific task and performs repetitive motions at high speed, hourly, daily and for months on end.

In 2016, 50,000 workers toiled away making Apple iPhones at the Pegatron factory in Shanghai. The hourly wage for these production workers was $2.00 ($1.85 after company deductions). Pegatron workers are also subject to monetary fines of between 5 and 10 percent of their base monthly wage for infractions such as wearing anti-static shoes outside or crossing their legs (China Labor Watch and The Future in Our Hands 2015). In short, wages are so low that workers must rely on overtime. Additionally, many young workers send a share of their wages, called remittances, home to support their rural families. This puts even more pressure on them to work longer hours.

A report issued by China Labor Watch sampled factory pay stubs and found that 78 percent of Pegatron workers worked more than 80 hours a month overtime (China Labor Watch 2016). A regular work week consists of 60 hours: 5 12-hour shifts with 50 minutes for lunch and 30 minutes for dinner. Workers stand at an assembly line building component parts of the iPhone. They must cover for each other – doing the job of two or three workers – when they take their meal breaks (China Labor Watch and The Future is in Our Hands 2015). More recently, due in part to a labor shortage and increasing worker resistance, Pegatron has had to rely less on forced overtime. As a result, it has tried to shift more costs for housing, meals and social insurance onto the workers (Oster 2016).

The example of Pegatron is emblematic of the international division of labor. Since the 1980s, with the rise of global competition and the adoption of neoliberal policies promoting free trade and open access to world markets, capitalist firms have sought new methods to sustain and grow their profits. The ability to move different stages of the production process to countries offering the lowest costs transformed the division of labor into a global phenomenon. Under the international division of labor, the manufacturing of clothing, toys, home appliances and consumer electronics takes place primarily in Southeast Asia, Latin America and China, where wages are low and there are plentiful supplies of workers. In turn, high-wage jobs associated with product development, research, financing and marketing are located in developed countries in North America, Britain and Europe.

In China, much of the industrial workforce consists of migrants arriving from rural provinces. Many of these workers have traditionally been young, single women. For example, one factory job posting read: "Only girls 18–35.

Obedient to management. Able to take hardship" (Blanding and White 2015). Factories provide sex-segregated dormitories adjacent to them for workers to live in. In some factories, workers are recruited from the same rural provinces and ethnic regions. On the one hand, this allows workers to form bonds with others from the same region or ethnic group. However, this also provides management with a way to divide the workforce along ethnic lines by pitting groups of workers against one another. For example, large factories have many separate production lines, and lines can be organized by ethnic group. At the end of a work shift, the volume of output assembled by each line is posted on a board. This tends to foment competition and division between production lines (Ngai 2007). As a result of this, workers are less likely to make alliances to resist management control over the production process. With dormitories on site, this control extends beyond the factory floor and into the personal lives of workers themselves. It also permits a more flexible use of labor since the proximity of workers makes them readily available to work if product demand suddenly increases.

For young workers separated from family and friends, working long hours, living in what amounts to a controlled environment with little or no privacy, the emotional toll can be great. In 2010, 18 Foxconn employees between the ages of 18 and 25 attempted suicide; 14 died while 4 survived with catastrophic injuries. One suicide survivor mentioned social isolation combined with harsh discipline and long hours spent on repetitive, physically stressful tasks as factors precipitating her decision to jump off the fourth floor of her dormitory. Safety nets have been installed at the dormitories to thwart further attempts at suicide. In a sense, these acts of desperation might also be interpreted as extreme forms of resistance to the low-road strategy adopted by a company squeezed to make cheaper products for transnational capitalist corporations (Chan and Pun 2010). The clustering of workers in dormitories also allows for the flow of information, including shared grievances about working conditions, and accounts of sexual abuse and the arbitrary use of discipline by managers. Thus, information-sharing holds the potential to build solidarity among workers and enable them to disrupt the production goals of the company (Smith and

Pun 2006). Indeed, the rise of large-scale industrial production employing millions of migrant workers has recently been accompanied by an increase in work stoppages and other forms of opposition to poor wages and working conditions in China (Leung 2015).

The low road is also a strategy of choice for many employers in developed countries, too. This is especially the case for low-wage, non-union work in the service sector. Consider the example of fast-food workers. Scientific management and assembly-line techniques have long been adopted in the fast-food industry. Workers in this industry are among the lowest paid of any occupation. The goal of the low road is to ensure high profits by keeping labor costs down and worker productivity up. As we have seen previously, this can be accomplished by increasing the length of the working day or by increasing the intensity of work per unit of time (more work effort per hour, for example). A Marxist analysis would characterize the extension of the work day as an example of increasing absolute surplus value, whereas increasing work effort per unit of time is consistent with increasing relative surplus value, where surplus value is the portion of labor in excess of the wages needed to reproduce the work force. The surplus then is the source of capitalist profit. So, in order to extract more profits from the workforce, employers engage in two additional strategies: (1) wage theft and (2) wage suppression.

Wage theft involves paying workers less than they are legally entitled to receive. Wage theft takes many different forms including:

- paying workers less than the minimum wage
- overtime work without additional overtime pay
- forcing workers to work more hours "off the clock" and therefore unpaid
- requiring workers to work through their meal or rest breaks
- taking all or a portion of workers' earned tips (in the United States, the minimum wage for restaurant waiting staff and other workers earning tips is $2.13 per hour, with employers expecting that customer tips should make up for these miserably low wages).

A recent report by the Economic Policy Institute estimated that US workers lose $64 per week ($3,300 per year) due to wage theft. One survey found that 17 percent of all low-wage workers are victims of wage theft (Cooper and Kroeger 2017). Wage theft can take other forms as well. For example, in Japan, young, first-time workers often accept jobs without knowing the level of pay or the number of hours they are expected to work. This has resulted in pressure for workers to put in long hours for prolonged periods of time. This pattern of overwork has even been linked to premature death and suicide (Adelstein 2017).

Finally, wage suppression is another low-road strategy whereby employers pay workers wages so low that they qualify for government assistance such as food aid. Employers can then shift part of the cost of reproducing labor onto the public, through the use of state subsidies intended to provide a minimum standard of living to the poor. In a highly publicized account, a McDonald's company-sponsored helpline included information advising workers to apply to the government's Supplemental Nutrition Assistance Program, also known as food stamps (Abad-Santos 2013). On a McDonald's website intended to provide financial guidance to employees struggling financially, the company advised that workers need two full-time jobs to make ends meet (Weissmann 2013). It is informative to note that the low-road strategy adopted by fast-food employers in the United States has been, by and large, successfully exported to Japan, Britain and Europe. As the world's largest employer in the fast-food sector, McDonald's has carefully avoided unionization, kept wages low, relied on hiring workers – students and migrant workers – who possess little economic and political power, enforced a strict regime of discipline, and engaged in the manipulation of work hours as a form of wage theft (Royle 2010).

From Low-Road to High-Road Strategies

If the low-road strategy sees wages as a cost of production, the high-road strategy focuses on the wage as a source of consumer demand. This corresponds more closely to the

Keynesian and Post-Keynesian perspectives within political economy. One of Keynes' major contributions to modern economics was to single out the role of demand in maintaining employment and economic growth. Demand comes from businesses, government, foreign countries and consumers. The focus of the high-road strategy identifies consumer demand resulting from workers' wage income as a key determinant of employment growth. This strategy also reflects a strand of Marxist economics that draws attention to the need for capitalism to avoid economic crises by ensuring sufficient demand to purchase the goods and services generated by capitalist producers. Inadequate levels of demand mean that goods are unsold so prices must be slashed, thereby reducing revenue and profits for employers. In Marxist terms, this illustrates a problem of underconsumption which leads to a crisis of realization, meaning that capitalist producers are unable to sell their products and therefore fail to realize or recover the full value of the products that they put up for sale. But the high road involves more than high and growing wages.

Glimpses of the high-road strategy can be seen in early twentieth-century attempts by capitalists to improve the working conditions and standard of living of their own employees. It was thought that a healthy and contented working class would also be more productive and less conflict-prone. Several employers, such as retailer Edward Filene in Boston, camera and optical equipment manufacturer George Eastman in Rochester, New York, and the Cadbury brothers' chocolate factories in Britain adopted this paternalistic approach toward managing their workforce (Nelson 1982; Dellheim 1987; Jacoby 1997). Their company policies included paying a living wage with health benefits, an on-site infirmary, and educational and cultural opportunities. The ideas and policies put in place acknowledged a relationship between a worker's experience of work and their willingness to work hard for the benefit of the company. It was intended to create loyalty by making workers feel they were valued members of the company family. Loyal workers were more likely to adopt company goals and comply with the company policies. They were also less likely to complain and less inclined to unionize. These paternalistic employers publicly announced concern for their workers' welfare. Their approach came to be known as welfare capitalism. Employers adopted this set of labor management practices at about the same time as other companies were using the drive system to squeeze more work out of their workforce via authority, strict discipline and fear. This pre-dated the rise of the welfare state. In fact, these employers believed that if all capitalists provided for the economic and social well-being of their workers, there might not be a need for government programs to raise worker standards of living and provide for their economic security.

One employer who combined elements of the drive system with a paternalistic approach toward the workforce was the Ford Motor Company. In 1914, Ford introduced a wage policy that doubled the existing daily wage from $2.50 to $5.00. But not all workers were able to qualify for $5 a day. Every worker needed to pass inspection by Ford staff. But inspectors did not evaluate how the worker performed on the job. Instead, they made house visits to investigate the workers' social, moral and cultural environment. Ford's "methods of work were thus linked to efforts to rationalize sexual, emotional, personal, and family life" (Steinmetz 1994, 187). This close supervision of workers' personal lives was one of the costs of working for Ford. The wage increase was referred to by the company as a profit-sharing plan. A firm's revenue is allocated either to wages or to profit. This is seen as a zero-sum game, meaning that, for a given level of revenue, every dollar that goes to wages must reduce profits by 1 dollar. So if workers were described as sharing in the profits of Ford Motor, it was clear that Ford's goal was to share a growing level of profits. This is known as a positive-sum game whereby each side shares the gains from increasing revenue. This does not mean that the gains are equally divided. Ford workers lacked a union to bargain collectively on their behalf. So the company had more power to set a level of wages that benefited them. In this way, the wage functions not as a payment to a resource input but as a strategic variable that employers can use to increase output.

First, the wage at Ford was higher relative to wages at other manufacturing companies. If workers lost their job at Ford, they would have to get a job at another company at a lower wage. This had an effect on the willingness of workers to stay on at Ford, reducing the number of workers who quit, thereby lowering the cost of hiring and training new workers. Also, high wages at Ford made workers willing to provide more effort in order to keep their job. This then had a direct effect on productivity. By standardizing the production process, Ford initiated a detailed division of labor – recall the Ford example of spring production. But the company also employed specialized machines that could perform repetitive tasks. These machines were enormous and expensive but, since the volume of production was so large – requiring 100,000 workers at one plant alone – the cost of machinery could be spread out over many cars, so the unit cost, and hence the price, of each car was lower than that of their competitors. Workers produced more cars in less time and Ford was able to thereby lower automobile prices, increase sales revenue and profit. This plan worked as long as there were consumers willing and able to buy Ford cars. Replicated by more and more companies, the system came to be known as Fordism, combining mass production with mass consumption (Aglietta 1979).

If employers were unwilling to voluntarily raise wages, workers were willing to organize unions to fight for wage increases. Companies that resisted unionization still felt pressure to match wage bargains made by their unionized competitors in order to forestall a union organizing their workforce. In this way, an economic regime characterized by rising real wages – wages that exceeded increases in the cost of living – came to define industrialized economies in the second half of the twentieth century. In addition, a system of income support for those who were unemployed or unable to work formed the foundation of the welfare state commitment to maintaining a basic standard of living. The positive-sum game benefited workers and employers, with many workers experiencing tangible improvements in their quality of life. However, it needs to be underscored that the primary beneficiaries were white, male workers, so the benefits were experienced unevenly by race and gender.

While Fordism originated in the United States, it eventually spread to Western European countries. Initially, the diffusion of Fordist mass production was impeded by the smaller market size of individual countries, together with lower wages for European auto workers. Only after the Second World War did Fordist techniques of production and workplace relations between capital and labor in Europe resemble the US model (Silver 2003). With the large-scale employment of workers came the elimination of skill differences through the transformation of manufacturing away from small-scale technology reliant on specialized craft workers toward the use of specialized machinery in combination with deskilled work. Labor–management conflict, strikes and work slowdowns illustrated the rising power of labor to disrupt production. The pattern of labor unrest took on distinct spatial and temporal patterns mirroring the spread of Fordist production, starting first in the United States and Canada (1930s and 1940s), then shifting to Britain (1950s) and Western Europe (1960s and 1970s), and then to the industrializing economies of Brazil, South Africa and South Korea (1980s and 1990s) (Silver 2003). It is important to note that this pattern reflected national differences in industrial relations laws and practices, and so should not be interpreted as simply the result of new technology and management practices. For example, the strength of Western European unions allowed for more bargaining power and coordination of production in some countries (e.g. German works councils). In other countries (e.g. Italy), the strategic use of strikes and increased voice of labor in determining production decisions had broader national political ramifications that went beyond the factory floor (Katz and Darbishire 2000; Hall and Soskice 2001; Silver 2003).

Beginning in the mid-1970s, the Fordist system was no longer able to return the level of profits that capitalists required. Several factors, including global competition, productivity slowdowns and spikes in natural resource prices, threatened the viability of Fordism. This then resulted in a series of shifts in the economic and political landscape that tilted the balance of power toward capitalists and away from workers. Some of those changes had direct effects on the workplace, and those changes influenced whether a high- or low-road strategy was adopted. Such changes included:

- The traditional mass production system whereby a single employer controlled the entire chain of production was replaced by outsourcing work to competing suppliers who were then responsible for producing products at the lowest cost. As a result, many of the supplier firms reverted to the use of the drive system, illustrated by the example of cell phone manufacturing.

- Making workers and work more flexible. This involved two types of flexibility:
  - Functional flexibility: Work was restructured so that workers performed multiple tasks, requiring them to have more, not fewer, skills. This also meant that they could perform more than one job, thereby allowing employers to shrink the size of their workforce.
  - Numerical flexibility: Fewer workers were hired as full-time workers. Instead, companies relied on temporary staff to work as needed on a project-by-project basis. Temporary workers did not qualify for company benefits such as health care or retirement pensions (Piore and Sabel 1984).
- Introduction of work teams whereby groups of workers collaborated in the production process. Collaboration took various forms, ranging from cooperation and task rotation to competition and aggressive monitoring of co-workers.
- Use of quality circles and continuous improvement, whereby workers are encouraged to suggest ways to streamline the production process. This was sometimes experienced by workers as a way to elicit their participation in the process of shrinking the workforce. In addition, the focus on continuous improvement placed stress on workers to push themselves beyond their physical and mental limits in order to continuously test those limits (Parker and Slaughter 1988).

Some of these managerial strategies – upgrading worker skills, involving workers in the production and design of workplace changes, team production – came to be identified with high-performance work organizations (Applebaum, Bailey, Berg and Kalleberg 2000; Osterman 2018). The high-performance label refers to the productivity gains and competitive advantage that resulted from the adoption of these workplace innovations. While the gains are sometimes associated with higher wages, this is not necessarily true across all industries (Osterman 2006). There is also mixed evidence that high-performance firms improve worker job satisfaction (Lloyd and Payne 2006).

Set against this backdrop of changes in the workplace were changes in management discourse and changes in the structure of the economy:

- The publication of the book *What Do Unions Do?* (Freeman and Medoff 1984) identified two major decisions that workers can make when confronting problems at work: (1) Exit or (2) Voice. "Exit" means quitting and finding another job. This is a fairly standard option for workers in the free-market economy: if you don't like your job, you can quit. What was eye-opening was the alternative to Exit: Voice. "Voice" means staying in your job but engaging in a dialogue with your employer about how to change things. But few workers would choose to confront their employers on their own for fear of being fired. What unions do is provide workers with a voice. Since a union represents a large group of workers, it would be more difficult for employers to fire a unionized worker without incurring a cost. Focusing on voice explains a counter-intuitive finding of this research – namely, that unionized workplaces are more likely to report dissatisfied workers. Once given a voice, workers are more likely to have grievances because they understand that they will be listened to. If workers have no hope that their situation will improve, they are less willing to voice their dissatisfaction.
- There was a slow but seismic shift in the structure of work in developed economies. Namely, manufacturing employment was shrinking because it was moving to lower-wage countries such as China and India. On the other hand, employment in service industries was growing. In 2017, there were eight service workers for every one manufacturing worker in the United States. In the UK, the ratio was nearly nine to one. But it is important to realize that the service sector is very diverse and includes occupations ranging from CEOs and doctors on the one end to home health aides and fast-food workers on the other. Also

there is wide variation across countries. For instance, in Germany and Italy the ratio is nearly four to one and in France it is six to one.[1]

So the adoption of high-road managerial strategies took place within this changing environment. High-road strategies are linked to high wages and improved working conditions. They sometimes involve a flattening of the corporate hierarchical structure. For example, some companies have adopted a rule that the top-paid executives can never earn more than x times the lowest-paid workers. So if management wants a raise, the wages of workers at the bottom must also rise. Additional high-road practices may include the creation of job ladders for workers. For example, in the restaurant industry, Restaurant Opportunity Center – a labor organization – works with restaurants to provide training for "back of the house" workers (for example, bussers, dishwashers) that will move them into jobs in cooking or "front of the house" service (Batt, Lee and Lakhani 2014). In Sweden, retail workers are offered training and certification of their skills in order to create career pathways to higher-wage jobs (Andersson, Kazemi, Tengblad and Wickelgren 2011).

At the risk of over-simplification, we can identify key differences between the low road and the high road. Low-road strategies characterize the workplace as a space in which conflict is the norm. This includes worker–manager conflict but it can extend to worker–worker conflicts based on ethnic or racial divisions established and maintained by employers to keep workers from organizing collectively. In addition, low-road strategies are predicated on keeping costs low and profits high. If low-road firms dominate the industrial landscape, then economic growth is largely profit-led. High-road strategies, by contrast, seek to establish wages as the source of economic growth, rather than profits. Furthermore, cooperation rather than competition is thought to be the norm to be used to elicit worker participation in improving the production process. High and growing wages lead to more consumer spending and therefore more economic growth. In spite of the differences in low- and high-road managerial strategies, a consistent principle throughout is the goal of expanded corporate profitability. So, even in the case of the high road, workers are expected to generate a growing surplus for their employer. Take the case of Google Inc. Most Google workers in the United States receive high wages and generous benefits (often including stock options), all in a superb working environment. Employees work on a lush, green campus where they can avail themselves of restaurant-quality food, free massages, laundry services, recreational facilities and opportunities to socialize. The expectation is that workers will choose to spend more time at their work-place, thereby voluntarily extending the length of their work day. The company also provides transportation to and from work in wi-fi enabled vans so that workers can log-in and work while on the way to the office (English-Lueck and Avery 2017). Indeed, while the use of electronic communication (e-mail, Skype) provides workers with more flexibility about where they choose to work – allowing them, for instance, to spend more time at home with their family – it also has the effect of erasing the line between work time and leisure (non-work) time (Gregg 2011).

Debate within political economy extends beyond the orga-nization of the workplace to include the tendency for capital-ism to experience systemic crises marked by falling profits, asset depreciation and mass unemployment. For example, Marxist crisis theory maintains that technological change through the increased use of labor-saving machinery tends to undercut the very source of profits, namely the labor of workers. The tendency for employers to replace workers with machinery through automation not only deprives workers of jobs but also drives down the rate of profit thereby igniting an economic crisis. Post-Keynesians understand economic crisis as the outcome of deficient demand for goods and ser-vices. Attempts to bolster demand through the extension of financial credit and increasing financialization of the economy only adds to the fragility of the system, thereby leading to asset speculation (for example, housing price bubbles) and eventual crisis (Minsky 1977; Stockhammer 2011; Stock-hammer and Stehrer 2011).

Furthermore, for Marxists, a wage-led growth regime may choke off capitalist investments in expanded production thereby initiating a squeeze on profits and an intensification of class conflict between workers and capitalists (Bhaduri and

Marglin 1990). A closely related crisis theory called the Social Structure of Accumulation or Regulation School maintains that capitalist institutions, regulatory structures governing private property, monopolies, labor–management relations and financial practices, provide an environment conducive to profit-making. However, these institutions also contain their own internal contradictions reflecting conflicts between workers and capitalists or competitive struggles between business factions (e.g. transnational corporations vs. small- and medium-sized enterprises). Over time, the contradictions and conflicts between groups erode the ability of the existing institutional structure to maintain a profitable environment and, as a result, an economic crisis ensues (Jessop 1990; Wolfson and Kotz 2010).

Off-Road: The Rise of Precarious Work

For most people today, work takes place within the broader context of the dominant neoliberal economy. Neoliberalism can be characterized by the encroaching presence of market criteria (price, profit, cost, benefit) in determining the provision and allocation of goods and services formerly produced by the public and made available to all citizens (health care, education, old-age pensions, housing). The neoliberal economy is also marked by the growing power of transnational capital to mine the global labor market for workers of varying skills, demographic characteristics and behavioral traits. In doing so, the current neoliberal workplace incorporates elements of low road and high road in the interest of corporate profitability.

This plays itself out in numerous ways but political economists and sociologists have identified the increasingly precarious nature of work. By precarity, we mean work that is characterized by uncertainty and contingency in terms of the length of service, level of pay and daily hours of work. For example, in response to the breakdown of Fordism, capitalist firms made increasing use of sub-contracted, temporary, flexible labor. The rise of "zero-hours" work is one example of precarity. A worker who has a zero-hours contract is not promised work but must be available to take work for whatever length of time is required, whenever it is offered. In 2015, nearly 12 percent of British businesses used these contracts. They are more likely to be used by larger businesses employing over 250 workers. Furthermore, the majority of zero-hours contracts are to be found in business administrative and support services, food and hospitality, health care and construction (Pyper and Brown 2017).

Three distinct but intersecting types of precarious work can be defined: (1) precarious professionals; (2) gig entrepreneurs; (3) immigrant, migrant and criminalized workers. Guy Standing characterizes these three, often conflicting, groups of precarious workers as: (1) highly educated, young workers who are unable to attain the status they were led to believe their human capital investment would provide; (2) children of working-class families who cannot attain the job security, income and social stability of their parents; and (3) migrants and minorities cut off from their homes and lacking citizenship rights (Standing 2014, 971–2). In addition, there are those individuals, usually racial minorities, often males, who carry a criminal record and thus are stigmatized, discriminated against and largely marginalized in the labor market (Pager, Western and Sugie 2009).

Increasing precarity among professionals took place as companies shed their permanent workforce in favor of the numerical flexibility that could be achieved via short-term and zero-hours contracts. This practice, whereby corporations outsource jobs to other companies or to workers acting on their own as independent contractors, has resulted in a fissured workplace (Weil 2014). The benefit to the corporation engaged in fissuring is that it no longer has direct responsibility over these workers. They become employees of another company or are self-employed. For example, it has been common practice for companies to outsource janitorial, security and landscaping services. Additionally, they can outsource payroll, accounting and employee benefits to independent companies. They are no longer responsible for the wages and benefits of those workers. They can then request bids from competing firms, resulting in competition to provide the service at lower costs and lower wages.

To illustrate further, we can explore the case of computer software professionals. In particular, consider the role of mobile computer applications – or app – developers. The occupational trend in app development is to de-link the worker from any long-term relationship with an employer. This increases precarity, but not for everyone. For example, freelance developers invited to join Gigster, a startup that curates talent for use on short-term projects for major corporations, can work on as many or as few projects as they want for top-paying companies. However, what about the majority of app developers who are not invited to join Gigster? The freelance economy for these educated professionals holds anxiety and uncertainty as much as the promise of autonomy and freedom. In the United States, for example, between 2010 and 2016, real annual wages for app developers in the top 10 percent of the pay scale rose by over $11,000. By contrast, the annual wage for the lowest 10 percent actually fell by over $1,500. At the lowest hourly wage of US$29, app developers are competing with workers in India, Pakistan and Ukraine willing to work for one-third of the US wage.[2] Yet another example involves package delivery services that increasingly use independent workers who then bear responsibility for on-time delivery and staffing their own jobs. Take the case of Don Lane, a 53-year-old courier delivering packages for Amazon, Marks & Spencer and other companies in need of package delivery. Don is paid only after he makes a successful delivery. DPD, the courier he works for, classifies him as self-employed, so he is responsible for finding a replacement if he cannot make deliveries or will face a £150 penalty. A diabetic, Don's delivery schedule, coupled with the fear of losing money if he failed to locate a replacement, forced him to cancel numerous medical appointments. Working while ill during the frantic Christmas delivery season, Dan died in January of 2017. DPD meanwhile earned over £100 million profit in 2016 (Booth 2018).

In many respects, the rise of the gig entrepreneur represents the truly off-road character of working in the neoliberal economy. For workers in the "gig economy," the employer–employee relationship no longer exists, or at least not quite in the same way. Instead, the individual worker seeks out jobs on a short-term basis. Consider the Lyft or MyTaxi driver. The means and materials of production – a reliable car, the ability to drive and effectively navigate the streets, insurance, gas and maintenance – are owned by the individual worker. In addition, the individual worker is responsible for generating demand for their service, setting their own hours and target income. We call these individuals entrepreneurs because they bear the risk of failure to maintain their capital asset (car) and they suffer the consequences from failing to generate demand through, for example, user service ratings. As a result it is not surprising that workers in the gig economy piece together multiple jobs that may include working part-time for a traditional employer as a sales clerk, food server or administrative support staff. Many gig workers find it necessary to offer a variety of individual services in order to generate a sufficient income. These jobs in turn form part of a low-wage ecosystem. For example, the role of furniture assembler is an occupation that depends on the demand for low-price unassembled furniture. The company TaskRabbit fills the role of the labor market in matching consumers with individual workers for projects including yard maintenance, pet care, moving and, of course, furniture assembly. On its website, the company makes its relationship very clear to workers (known as Taskers): "Taskers on the platform are not employees of TaskRabbit; rather, they are independent contractors. Taskers set their own hourly rates for work, set their own schedules, and determine their own work areas."[3] The Swedish furniture company IKEA recently purchased TaskRabbit (Chaudhuri and Brown 2017).

Precarious labor is a characteristic of work throughout the world. In China, a large proportion of the urban workforce consists of migrants from rural villages recruited by agents seeking to find workers for construction and factory jobs, like the Pegatron and Foxconn workers discussed earlier. In the booming construction industry, Chinese workers can be hired on one-year contracts. The employer pays the cost of travel to the city and provides housing and food on the construction site itself. Wages, on the other hand, are withheld until the end of the year-long contract. The construction site on which workers live is literally walled off from the rest of the city and invisible to permanent city residents (Swider 2015). A different version of this system has contractors living near migrants from the same rural village or region, using social and kinship ties to bind the workers to the contractor over time and across work projects. Yet another form of precarious work common in China, the United States and many other countries is the spot labor market in which day laborers seek work by assembling at a particular place in the city where potential employers pass by in search of workers. This is the epitome of contingent work characterized by uncertainty (will I get a job today?), low wages, frequent wage theft and the threat of violence by employers who know workers have no legal recourse to report them to government authorities (Theodore, Valenzuela Jr. and Meléndez 2009; Swider 2015).

One issue arising from precarious work is whether these workers – the precariat – constitute a new class substantively different from the traditional, contractually employed working class. Is the precariat another version of the secondary labor market? Or is it a harbinger of a new structure for employment relations in the twenty-first century? The argument that the precariat represents a new class is based on the recognition that precarious work is inherently insecure in relation to employment / working conditions / income / community networks / access to skill development / legal status (Standing 2011). An alternative assessment maintains that, while precarity has always been a defining feature of work under capitalism, the contemporary neoliberal regime expanded the number of precarious jobs (Jonna and Foster 2016). The system of temporary, low-wage, unregulated, insecure employment in some ways represents a return to the experience of workers in the midst of the British industrial revolution chronicled by Marx. In describing the experience of the reserve army of labor, consisting of workers subject to frequent periods of unemployment, Marx identified floating, latent and stagnant sectors of the unemployed. The floating unemployed were those, mainly older males, who lost their jobs due to mechanization and were forced to seek out a series of increasingly temporary jobs. The latent segment consisted of those who moved from agricultural to factory jobs. The stagnant portion of the reserve army of labor consisted of workers whose employment is "extremely irregular" and whose living standards are far below those of the average worker (Marx 1977, 796).

Other political economists, while acknowledging the historical existence of flexible, temporary and informal work, also recognize the changing context of employment, away from the Fordist model of formal contracts, health and retirement benefits and labor market regulations (e.g. health and safety) toward new norms embodied in flexible, contingent and precarious work. They also note that these new forms of work require the development of alternative institutions and regulations aimed at protecting an increasingly vulnerable and exploited workforce (Peck and Theodore 2012). For instance, in place of traditional unions, "worker centers" have emerged on the scene in order to regularize employment by establishing more equitable hiring practices, assisting workers in combating wage theft, and providing education and skill development that create rungs on a career ladder so that workers can advance to stable, higher-wage jobs (Theodore, Valenzuela Jr. and Meléndez 2009).

Resistance to precarious work also takes the form of new global partnerships of organized labor. Building cleaners are emblematic of low-wage precarious labor found in countries around the globe. For example, Copenhagen-based International Service System (ISS) employs over 490,000 workers across Europe, Asia and the Americas. In 2016, it generated revenue of over 12 billion dollars (International Service System 2016). ISS provides janitorial, property maintenance, security and catering services to companies in airlines, health care, food service, hotels and leisure, and the retail trade. The occupations supported by these industries are among the fastest growing and lowest paid. Traditional unions have found it difficult to organize services. But the Service Employees International Union (SEIU) adopted the non-traditional organizing model as opposed to the more common service model. In the service model, the union's primary focus is on representing the interests of its current members. As the economy stagnated and corporate profits were squeezed in the late 1970s and early 1980s, employers in manufacturing took a hard-line stand against wage increases by threatening massive layoffs and plant closures. Unions seeking to protect their members' jobs bargained for wage concessions, effectively agreeing to wage cuts. But these concessions failed to stop companies from downsizing and moving jobs to low-wage countries. As a result, union membership shrank. This sparked efforts by unions to develop alternative strategies, such as the organizing model. In the organizing model, the line between organizing new workers and serving existing members is erased. Instead, the organizing campaign dovetails with contract negotiations and services to members. One of the key features of this model is the recognition that laborers have natural allies in the communities to which they belong. Demands for workplace justice – better pay, work–life balance, improved medical benefits, non-discriminatory hiring practices – have direct impacts on the lives of people outside of the workplace. So the SEIU organizing model sought to build partnerships with community organizations. This had the effect of expanding the terrain upon which negotiations took place. Community groups put pressure on employers by taking the union message into the community (Voss and Sherman 2000). Tactics included shaming the CEO and Board of Directors by, for example, publicly and often theatrically protesting in front of the company owner's home or attending Board of Director meetings to create public awareness of the union position. The SEIU successfully mounted such a large-scale effort in Los Angeles in the 1990s, through the Justice for Janitors campaign. As part of the campaign, SEIU representatives flew to ISS headquarters in Copenhagen to put pressure on the company. Later, in 2004, the SEIU formally adopted a policy aimed at internationalizing the scope of organizing by partnering with unions in other countries such as Ireland, Australia and Great Britain. In this way, global union cooperation, including a shared model of organizing and bargaining, represents an effective way of combating corporate power in the neoliberal era (Aguiar 2016).

Yet another off-road strategy used to organize work involves workers managing the production process collectively, without the need for employers. Take, for example, a house cleaner faced with these options: (1) working under contract for a house cleaning company; (2) working as an independent house cleaner in the gig economy; or (3) working as a live-in domestic worker for a private family with no contract or benefits. A fourth option is the worker cooperative in which workers band together to form a business enterprise owned and operated by the workers themselves. This is the idea behind the Women's Collective of the San Francisco Day Labor Program. In this example, day laborers performing house cleaning formed La Collectiva, a worker-run organization that provides cleaning services using environmentally safe products. In addition, collective members meet weekly to:

> develop strategies for ensuring health and safety in the domestic work industry, promote access to environmentally safe jobs, distribute information on toxic chemicals in cleaning products, discuss workplace ergonomics, and participate in other workshops and trainings. English and computer classes are designed to provide the predominantly immigrant population with the skills and information they need to raise awareness and resist workplace exploitation and abuse. The Collective's popular education strategy is designed to be peer-led and participatory, presenting another opportunity to build leadership and share information. The Collective also serves as a center of organizing around immigration issues, mobilizing workers and their advocates in response to recent waves of Immigration and Customs Enforcement raids against unauthorized workers. (Kennedy 2010, 153)

So the example of worker collectives and cooperatives offers a different way to structure work and to connect work with education, community organizing and political engagement. This cooperative model of work is explored in the next chapter.

5
Beyond Managerial Strategies: Worker Cooperatives

Origins of the Cooperative Movement

While the current organization of work appears timeless, something that will never change, it is important to remember that there are alternative ways to structure work. The cooperative economic ideal – that individuals desire to share equally in the rational organization of production – has a long legacy that parallels the history of capitalism. Workers in early nineteenth-century Britain confronted a brutal system of industrial manufacturing. Such was the quest for profits on the part of capitalists that for any individual worker it was virtually impossible to hold wages above starvation levels. Marx, writing about this period, explained that the "Accumulation of wealth at one pole is, therefore, at the same time, accumulation of misery, the torment of labour, slavery, ignorance, brutalization and moral degradation at the opposite pole" (Marx 1977, 799). Workers who sought to form unions risked being fired, labeled troublemakers and blacklisted by other employers. Such were the conditions when, in 1844, a small band of London weavers formed the Rochdale Society of Equitable Pioneers. The objectives of the Rochdale Pioneers were to: (1) open a cooperative store to sell clothing, flour, sugar, butter and oatmeal; (2) provide housing to members and their families; and (3) "commence the manufacture of such articles as the Society may determine upon, for the employment of such members as may be without employment, or who may be suffering in consequence of repeated reductions in their wages" (Holyoake 1893, 12).

The Rochdale Pioneers' cooperative store began with small weekly payments, known as subscriptions, from approximately 40 weavers. When a sufficient amount of funds was raised the weavers leased a building and began to purchase goods to sell. The goods were available to everyone in the neighborhood. There was an incentive for members of the cooperative to purchase at the store since the "profits" – revenue net of costs – were redistributed to the members. Instead of running up a debt with the local merchant, Rochdale cooperative members were now earning money by shopping at the cooperative store (Holyoake 1893). As the membership increased, its reputation as an institution promoting the well-being of the working class also grew:

> The members of the Store are so numerous, that the masters come in contact with them at almost every turn. The co-operators work for nearly every employer in the town, and many hold the most trusty and responsible situations. The working class in general hold the Co-operative Society in high esteem, and what is more natural, since it aims at bettering their condition. Indeed, the Society exercises considerable influence in the town. (Holyoake 1893, 27)

The early nineteenth-century cooperative movement in Britain developed as a direct challenge to industrial capitalism. The challenge took the form of a refutation of the claim that work organized around the goal of profit-making was the only way to manage commercial and industrial enterprises. As the historian E. P. Thompson describes the cooperative movement at that time, "It was in Lancashire and Yorkshire that we find the most rapid development of a *general theory* of a new 'system,' whereby on a national scale equitable exchange might take place, as well as some of the hardiest and most practical support for 'utopian' experiments in community-building" (1966, 792).

While the Rochdale cooperatives expanded to include weavers producing their own goods for sale, the establishment of a single consumer cooperative had an impact on the lives of the workers that extended beyond the mere buying of foodstuffs and clothing and sharing in the profits. It made a difference in the economic conditions of the workers in Rochdale. Similarly, a change in the organization of the economy can alter the way we perceive and act. The Rochdale weavers, having been presented with the option of shopping at a cooperative, may then have a preference to shop there, whereas before they did not because such alternatives were not on offer. This is a major tenet of political economy captured in the arcane academic phrase "endogenous preferences." What this means is that our preferences are shaped by the structure of the economy, such that "economic institutions may induce specific behaviors – self-regarding, opportunistic, or cooperative, say – which then become part of the behavioral repertoire of the individual" (Bowles 1998, 80). So, in this sense, our values and choices are inextricably tied up with our understanding of what is possible and attainable. And, furthermore, the workplace, where many people spend much of their time, shapes the values, tastes and preferences that people have. This notion of endogenous – inside the economy – preferences supports the notion that work is a realm of political and economic life where we learn the technical requirements of producing things at work but we also learn about justice/injustice, fairness/unfairness and the application of democratic/undemocratic principles.

The example provided by the original consumer cooperatives was extended to the producer or worker cooperative. Experiments in nineteenth-century worker cooperatives varied in structure and purpose and were often aligned with religious projects involving the moral development of the working class. They were organized in a paternalistic way, the most notable example being the cooperative communities established by Robert Owen in Britain and then in the United States. These relatively short-lived projects were characterized by Marx and Engels as examples of a utopian socialism that was different from scientific socialism in that scientific socialism would come about only after the full development of capitalist technology and productive capabilities. As such, for Marx, these nineteenth-century experiments with cooperatives were an interesting attempt to imagine what socialism may (or may not) look like, but they were destined to fail so long as capitalism continued to expand, mature and evolve.

Yet, from another vantage point, Marx was sympathetic to the radical critique of capitalism embodied in the practice of cooperative labor. For instance, citing an 1866 magazine article on the creation of a company in which owners would share a portion of the profits with their workers, Marx quotes from the story, "They showed that associations of workmen could manage shops, mills and almost all forms of industry with success, and they immensely improved the condition of the men, but then they did not leave a clear place for masters" (*Spectator* 1866, 569). To this, Marx retorts "*Quelle horreur!*" ("How awful!"). So, from this perspective, Marx looked favorably upon cooperatives created by workers as foreshadowing potential elements of a post-capitalist society. So we can say that, on the topic of worker cooperatives, Marx was for *and* against (Jossa 2005).

Worker Participation Versus Worker Control

Many types of participatory work organizations exist. They include traditional union–management collective bargaining which gives workers a collective voice in the determination of pay and benefits, along with a role in creating safe and healthy working conditions. The German model of co-determination, through which workers are represented on the board of directors where they participate in decisions over pay and production, is yet another form of participatory management (Streeck 1995). But participation has also been ascribed to profit-sharing plans and employee ownership of company stock (Employee Stock Ownership Plans or ESOPs), through which workers receive a share of profits or an equity stake in the company. These types of participatory workplaces conform to the high-road managerial strategy discussed in the previous chapter. Through shared decision-making, even going so far as giving workers the ability to decide on their compensation plan, worker productivity and firm profitability tend to increase (Mellizo, Carpenter and Matthews 2017). Yet in none of these examples do workers control the day-to-day decision-making in the firm, nor do they have majority ownership of the company's assets.

The separation of participation from control and ownership of the firm is an important distinction that separates a high-road managerial strategy from a worker-owned cooperative. The high-road participatory workplace does not challenge the authority of the owner. Furthermore, managers are employees who work at the behest and direction of the owner. So when high-road strategies come in conflict with the goal of profitability they can be curtailed or abandoned (Jenkins 2007; Butler, Glover and Tregaskis 2011). Consider the case of the New Belgium Brewing in Colorado. In 2013, the company became employee-owned through an ESOP. This means that the company's stock was owned by the workers themselves. However, the company was still controlled and owned by the founder and CEO, Kim Jordan. In 2018, the brewery laid off 28 workers. The rationale given was "As an employee-owned business, it is the executive team's responsibility to look out and make sure that their (employees) [*sic*] share value is being protected" (Funari 2018). Since the workers own the company stock, the value of shares took priority over the jobs of 28 of the "worker-owners." By contrast, the goal of worker-owned cooperatives, going all the way back to the Rochdale Pioneers, is to sustain and grow job opportunities in times of economic prosperity and to maintain employment in the face of economic downturns. Empirical studies also confirm that worker cooperatives provide more stable employment over the business cycle (Craig and Pencavel 1992; Burdin and Dean 2009).

The economic implication of the priority given to employment over profits is key to understanding worker cooperatives as a distinct alternative to business as usual. Post-Keynesian economists, for example, argue the benefit of maintaining full employment as a way of securing sufficient demand for goods and services. But full employment also shifts the balance of power from capital to labor (Kalecki 1943). Without the threat of job loss (unemployment), workers would be disinclined to provide surplus labor for their employers. A full-employment economy would be incompatible with the structure of capitalism since, as Keynes noted, involuntary unemployment was an abiding feature of the capitalist economy and the rule rather than the exception. This view runs counter to mainstream economics which maintains that full employment is the intended outcome of rational, self-interested buying and selling of labor in the market. As Kalecki argued, "Full employment capitalism will, of course, have to develop new social and political institutions which will reflect the increased power of the working class. If capitalism can adjust itself to full employment, a fundamental reform will have been incorporated in it. If not, it will show itself an outmoded system which must be scrapped" (1943, 5).

Political Structure of the Workplace

In volume I of *Capital*, Marx describes the capital–labor relationship in stark terms by contrasting the workplace to the mythical character of the free market. Upon leaving the marketplace and entering the workplace, Marx states:

> we think we can perceive a change in the physiognomy of our dramatis personae. He, who before was the money-owner, now strides in front as capitalist; the possessor of labour-power follows as his labourer. The one with an air of importance, smirking, intent on business; the other, timid and holding back, like one who is bringing his own hide to market and has nothing to expect but – a hiding. (Marx 1887/2015, 123)

The structure that governs the relationships between employer and employee is one in which power is centralized and used either to enforce discipline or to coax cooperation out of workers. In place of this autocratic system of governance, the worker cooperative strives to substitute democratic principles.

The core feature of a worker cooperative is the principle that every worker is a member of the firm and membership conveys voting rights involving the management of the firm. The workers are also owners and must contribute to the maintenance of the capital stock. In return worker-owners receive labor income in the form of wages and residual earnings that would otherwise be designated as profits in a traditional capitalist firm (Ellerman 1990). Small firms producing relatively simple products can be self-managed if workers take collective responsibility for supervising one another. However, as the volume of production increases and the technical process of production gets more complex, there will presumably need to be a separate class of managers to oversee the work. But since the workers collectively own the enterprise, the workers elect managers who are themselves members of the cooperative. Additional governing bodies consisting of worker members may also be established to facilitate communication between different divisions of the company, take decisions on behalf of the members, and oversee the provision of social benefits such as health care, education and training opportunities. The representatives are elected from the ranks of the members, serve a fixed term and can be replaced by a vote of the members.

A serious issue confronting worker-owned cooperatives is the need for capital investment. If worker-owned firms are expected to compete in a capitalist economy, then they need access to funds necessary to invest in maintaining and replacing equipment, and purchasing new technology. If internal funds are not available, firms need access to external funding from banks or private investors. On the one hand, banks may be less willing to lend to worker cooperatives because the cooperative's commitment to maintain employment at the expense of profitability runs counter to traditional capitalist business practices. As such, they will fail to conform to the criteria implemented by banks to assess risk and therefore lending would appear more risky. In addition to risk assessment, private investors expect to exert control over business decisions and this contradicts the democratic principles of enterprises owned and managed by the workers (Gintis 1989; Major 1996).

On the other hand, there are equally vexing problems associated with self-financing by using contributions from worker members. If individuals lend money to (or invest in) the firm, they may be more interested in taking decisions that ensure that their investment will pay off, even if those decisions are at odds with the broader economic goals of the cooperative. This is especially the case if workers do not contribute an equal share of their income to the investment fund. As a result, many cooperatives use investment accounts for each member along with a larger social investment fund created from a portion of the surplus revenue generated that would have otherwise gone to profits in a capitalist firm

(Gunn 2011). It is important to note that there is no generic blueprint for how to organize a cooperative workplace. The local/national culture, legal regulations and political environment all act to shape the organizational structure of a cooperative firm.

Worker Control of the Firm Versus Worker Control of the Economy: Mondragon

The question of whether worker-owned cooperatives are sustainable gets to the heart of the debate over cooperatives. While the principles that govern worker cooperatives – democratic decision-making, one member one vote, collective ownership, employment maintenance prioritized over layoffs, equitable sharing of the surplus revenue produced, managers who are hired by members and who are cooperative members – are markedly different than the practices used by capitalist firms, an individual cooperative has to compete with capitalist firms in local, national and global markets. Those that are successful and long-lived are often small and serve a relatively local market (for example, day-care centers, bookstores and restaurants) or they are able to produce unique products that develop and nurture relations with cooperatives throughout the supply chain (for example, fair-trade coffee and chocolate). But there are examples of successful, mature cooperatives that have developed networks of mutual support and cooperation within a specific geographic region. As a result, this regional economy of cooperatives produces positive effects that extend beyond a single workplace (Smith 2003). These effects may range from reassigning workers to other cooperatives from plants that are suffering from low product demand to sharing research and development, training and social service (e.g. health care, child care) facilities. Perhaps the most well-known example of a successful regional cooperative system is called Mondragon in the Basque region of Spain.

The Mondragon cooperatives began in 1956 with one 23-member firm producing cooking stoves. Recent estimates put Mondragon's employment at about 60,000 workers in over 100 cooperatives in Spain along with an additional 12,000 global non-member employees. As many as 43 percent of Mondragon employees live in the Basque country while another 40 percent live elsewhere in Spain (Mondragon Corporation 2017). Today, a worker who joins the Mondragon cooperative can find employment in one of four sectors: industry, finance, retail and knowledge (education, training and research). The Mondragon system consists of primary cooperatives producing goods such as automotive parts, batteries, robotics and automation systems, machine tools, medical equipment, bicycles and language translation and training services to meet demand in local, national and international markets. In addition, secondary-level cooperatives support the primary industrial cooperatives. Secondary cooperatives include schools and technical training facilities, a cooperative bank, health care services, insurance and retirement services. In most workplaces, wages are set in accordance with a rule by which the ratio of lowest- to highest-paid employee is 1:5, although they can go as high as 1:8.9 (Arando, Freundlich, Gago, Jones and Kato 2011, 261). Compare this to the 271:1 ratio between the wage of the average US CEO and the typical worker (Mishel and Schieder 2017).

Upon joining the cooperative, a worker is required to pay a membership fee and to contribute to an individual capital account. This allows the firm to finance its operations without relying on outside investors. At the end of the year, profits are credited to a worker's capital account. The worker can withdraw their money after they leave the firm or retire (Ellerman 1990). Another portion of profits is retained in the reserve fund and yet a third portion is contributed to a pool to which all the cooperatives contribute. This "solidarity fund" is used to assist cooperatives that are suffering slowdowns. A final portion of profits is set aside for education and training activities (Arando, Freundlich, Gago, Jones and Kato 2011, 263). These last two functions – assisting firms in distress, and support for education and training – are especially important to workers who lose their job. Unlike the capitalist firm, a single cooperative or a single-industry cooperative, a regional economy populated by a diverse mix of cooperatives is able to absorb displaced workers into other firms and industries. Even in the face of an economy-wide recession, the cooperative system is able to maintain employment for most workers. For example, in the immediate aftermath of the economic crisis of 2008, only 200 of Mondragon's workers were without a job. But even then, those workers were still earning 80 percent of their regular wages (Arando, Freundlich, Gago, Jones and Kato 2011, 249).

Mondragon's governance structure is organized around a large all-member governing body, a working group – the Governing Council – and two additional representative groups for management – the Management Council – and shop-floor workers – the Social Council (Figure 5.1). Workers participate through their membership in the General Assembly. The General Assembly decides on budgets, resource allocation and major changes in the operation of the cooperative. Everyone is expected to participate in the General Assembly meetings once or twice a year. Here worker members vote to elect representatives to the Governing Council. A worker

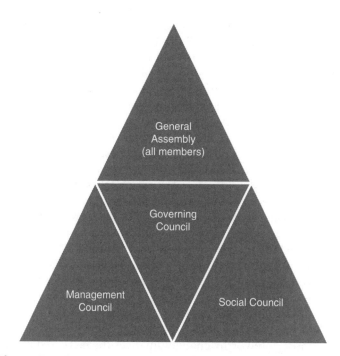

Figure 5.1 Governance structure of Mondragon cooperatives

elected to the Governing Council is involved in week-to-week approval of management decisions and policies. Members of the Governing Council have responsibility for monitoring the performance of the management and must approve all managerial appointments. Representatives from management are ratified by the Governing Council to serve on a Management Council.

The Social Council is also an elected body that functions to maintain communication between the shop-floor workers and the management. It was envisioned as a body that most effectively represents the interests and concerns of the workers directly involved in the production process. For example, one goal of the Social Council is to participate in the design and implementation of alternatives to the monotonous, deskilling assembly-line jobs found in capitalist-owned firms. In some ways, the Social Council is similar to a union to the extent that it provides shop-floor workers an independent voice in determining the organization of the workplace. However, by participating too closely with managers, Social Council members are open to criticism of being co-opted by management (Whyte and Whyte 1988, 123–4; Latinne 2014).

The decision-making structure, while hewing closely to the democratic principle of one member one vote, is flexible enough to allow for differences. For example, Alecop is a technical training and education cooperative. It began in 1966 and its students take classes for four hours and then work four hours in an industrial plant. One of the first customers for Alecop products were schools seeking to purchase instruments and measurement devices to use in science and engineering classes. Today, Alecop matches students with companies interested in recruiting new workers and developing their skills. It also allows students to initiate classroom projects in a cooperative firm setting. The participants in Alecop include faculty, students and company employees who supervise the students at work. As a result, one-third of the governing council is elected by the staff and faculty, one-third by the students, and one-third by the contracting companies (Whyte and Whyte 1988, 54; Alecop Group n.d.).

What has changed since Mondragon began in 1956? One of the most noteworthy changes involves the increased global competition facing Mondragon products. As a result, the cooperative opened manufacturing facilities outside of Spain. The workers at most of these new firms are not members of the cooperative. In addition, temporary workers under contract with Mondragon firms are also non-members. Recent data indicate that about 78 percent of Mondragon's industrial workforce is comprised of cooperative members (Mondragon Corporation 2016). This leads us to consider a final debate over the role of cooperatives in the economy. Cooperatives can transform the world of work, especially if they are part of a diverse network of linked companies and workplaces. The regional cooperative represents an alternative workplace in which democratic principles, worker control over production and worker ownership of the firm result in a more equal distribution of income and more stable employment compared to the work in the capitalist firm. Mondragon is perhaps the best example of a regional cooperative. However, the argument against cooperatives has been that, aside from the integrated, large-scale regional cooperatives like Mondragon, cooperatives are too often small and disconnected from the type of secondary-level support institutions, especially financial and business support services, necessary to remain viable. In this view, capitalist firms are too powerful and until the economic system itself is radically restructured cooperatives will continue to play a minor role. In response to this argument, political economists have put forth an alternative vision of the economy referred to by several different names: solidarity economy, community economies and participatory economics.[1]

Cooperative Work in Solidarity and Community Economies

Instead of seeing the economy as a place in which everyone works for a wage in a profit-making company – like the workers in the British and US television show *The Office* – the community economies perspective views the economy as diverse. In addition to the traditional capitalist wage-labor economy there are other economies: family economies, non-profit economies, sharing economies and cooperative economies, to name a few. In fact, one can argue that by only thinking of the economy as corporate, capitalist, hierarchical and authoritarian, we overlook a lot of the other workplaces in which people participate every day. It is as if we see only the tip of the iceberg. In fact, the proponents of the community economies approach frequently represent the economy as an iceberg (Figure 5.2). Here we can see that

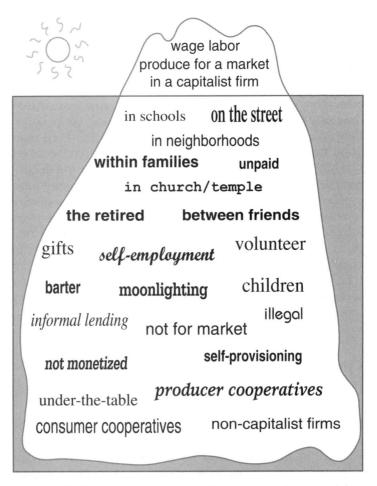

Figure 5.2 Diverse types and sites of work: capitalist wage labor as the tip of the iceberg
Source: K. Byrne, www.communityeconomies.org/Home/Key-Ideas

cooperatives – both consumer cooperatives and producer/ worker cooperatives – are two among several different ways to participate in the economy. If we step back and understand work as involving more than simply wage labor, the world of work is all around us: in families, at school, in voluntary and religious organizations, in gift-giving and in non-profit social service and cultural agencies.

Similarly, the solidarity economy and participatory economics approaches also attempt to highlight the non-capitalist features of economic life. This extends beyond the world of work to include consumption and exchange of services and material goods. For example, in communities in Canada, Argentina, Britain and the United States, unemployment, underemployment and low incomes combined to create a need for new systems of production and exchange. Local exchange trading systems arose to meet the needs of community members who had skills and time but no employment. A system of labor exchange based on individual accounts measured in labor time or using local alternative currencies tied to a recognized unit of labor time (e.g. 1 hour of labor = \$15) allowed individuals to buy and sell goods and services to one another without the need for an employer or a retail store (North 2007). Furthermore, the fair and ethical trade movements involve individual consumers in the work of evaluating the conditions under which products are made. The US company Equal Exchange, for example, is run as a producer and consumer cooperative that seeks to promote agricultural cooperatives internationally and domestically (Brown and Getz 2008; Raynolds 2009). These examples allow us to begin to view work in a broader social and economic landscape. This is going to become more important in the future as the world of work is increasingly affected by changes in technology leading some political economists to think about the world of work beyond (and after) paid labor.

6

Technology, Automation and Skills: Restructuring the Workplace

The Technology Debate

The effect of the introduction of new technology on work has been the subject of much debate in political economy. New technology holds forth the promise of increased efficiency and labor productivity. With technological improvements comes a rising standard of living. New machinery also enhances the quality of working life through the elimination of monotonous or hazardous jobs and the development of new skills associated with controlling and producing the new technology. On the other hand, new machines and automated production processes can threaten established ways of making a living, render skilled craftsmanship obsolete and reduce worker wages. The benefits may be siphoned off by the owners of the patents and the corporate executives who extract economic rents from their monopoly control over the new technology.

While mainstream economists today may lament the fact that some workers suffer job loss as the result of the introduction of new technology – think robots and automation – they nevertheless believe that this is short-term, localized misfortune. As the new technology becomes widely adopted, the demand for workers to produce it will increase. So, workers thrown out of work by machines can find work producing the very machines that displaced them. Alternatively, workers can find new jobs in other industries because the new technology allows employers to produce products at lower cost. As a result the demand for these products will rise or the demand for other products will increase as buyers who purchase the same amount of the cheaper product will have money left over to buy other goods. In turn, the demand for labor will rise. This explanation has a long history going back several hundred years when it was known as the compensation theory (Vivarelli 2014). Marx harshly criticized this theory for several reasons. First, the number of workers absorbed by the machine-producing sector will fall short of the workers made unemployed through its introduction. Also, the addition of these displaced workers to the army of the unemployed will depress wages for those workers who can find alternative lines of work. Overall, Marx thought that the impact on workers would be devastating: "Crippled as they are by division of labour, these poor devils are worth so little outside their old trade, that they cannot find admission into any industries, except a few of inferior kind, that are over-supplied with underpaid workmen" (Marx 1887/2015, 294). Yet, since new machinery is profitable when it is first introduced by the innovative firm, other firms will be compelled to adopt it. Indeed, for Marx, the development of the tools, machines and technologies of production – what he calls the "means of production" – is imperative in order for capitalism to grow and expand. Yet a contradiction arises when the very source of profit, the surplus value produced by workers over and above their wages, decreases as fewer and fewer workers are required in the automated factories. While this contradiction introduces a crisis for capitalism, it also suggests an alternative world in which laboring for someone else is no longer necessary.

Early Industrial Conflict Over Machine Production

Opposition to machine production took different forms in different countries. In the late eighteenth century, feudal families and aristocrats received special exemptions from taxes and regulations in order to promote the creation of industrial enterprise zones in the French textile-producing region of Normandy. The goal was to encourage the production of high-quality fabrics to export at low costs. The spinning machine was introduced as a way to produce cheaper quality fabrics without the need to hire craft workers. The textile spinners who remained, the majority of whom were women, saw their wages fall due to the lower cost of using machines. One spinning machine or frame could do the work of 100 workers (Horn 2012, 177). As one writer at the time exclaimed, "These fine machines will enrich a few individuals, but will ruin a whole country" (Manuel 1938, 181).

By 1789, with rising unemployment in the Normandy region, the tide turned. The workers of Normandy took to the streets, marching toward manufacturers who employed machines with the intent of destroying them. From July through October, battles were waged, machines were burned. Employers and police retaliated with force, killing many protesters (Horn 2012, 179–83). It is important to recognize that this was no one-sided reaction against machinery. Workers in Normandy opposed the introduction of machinery because it foreclosed the possibility for a different kind of economy based on fair prices, employment for all who wanted work, and decent wages. Workers in the region clamored for an inward-looking system of production that met local and regional needs while privileging workers over the use of machine technology (Horn 2012). Around three decades later, British workers rose up against the real threat of starvation resulting from both the elimination of state protections like the minimum wage and the introduction of labor-replacing machinery. The workers, known as Luddites, engaged in numerous acts of destruction of machines and raw materials, partly as a way to agitate for better wages – a form of "collective bargaining by riot" (Hobsbawm 1964, 7). Rather than seeing these movements as futile efforts that simply postponed the inevitable adoption of machinery, a political economy perspective recognizes that the adoption of technology involves the restructuring of workplaces along with a reordering of the balance of power between employers and employees. In these historical examples, workers wanted to preserve a set of traditions and values that represented a fairer, more humane, moral economy (Thompson 1966, 1971).

Political Economy Approaches to Technological Change

Writing during the last half of the nineteenth century, Marx had a unique vantage point from which to assess the impact of technology on work. While he was sympathetic to the effects of technological change on the lives of working people, he believed that the Luddites and machine-breakers in general were mistaken to channel their anger and resentment at the machines instead of the "form of society which utilizes those instruments" – namely, capitalism (Marx 1977, 555). Yet Marx also acknowledged the destructive effect of machinery on the lives of workers. This includes workers who lose their jobs as a result of new technology, as well as workers able to hold on to their jobs. For employed workers, the impact of new technology weakens their bargaining power. Marx reflected that, "It would be possible to write a whole history of the inventions made since 1830 for the sole purpose of providing capital with weapons against working-class revolt" (Marx 1977, 563). Technology should be seen as more than simply a means by which to produce more goods at a lower cost. Its introduction and the resistance to it reflect political as well as economic interests. So the French and English opposition to machinery was both a reaction against an economic system in which workers and machines were interchangeable and a call for an alternative organization. It was possible to imagine more than one single technology that could produce more goods at lower cost. This is the story that underlies the theory of path-dependent technological change. According to this view, technologies compete with one another and the best technique may or may not emerge triumphant. So, the system of work we have today may not be the most productive. In fact, Marxist political economists argue that production technologies and work organizations are selected and adopted not because they are the most productive but because they maintain control of the factory and generate profits for the owners of the company (Marglin 1974; Bowles 1985; Nuvolari 2002).

The political economy debate over the impact of technological change includes the Post-Keynesian view that the adoption of new technology can create extra profits – also called economic rents – for the initial adopters, which, if labor unions exist and are sufficiently powerful, can be shared with workers. The higher wages can lead to increased demand for goods and services. Furthermore, if the new technology has broad use and can be widely adopted across industries, then this can bring about economic growth and with it added demand for labor. Finally, if new technology takes the form of new products – think of the automobile and the computer – and these products either generate demand for complementary goods – suburban housing in the case of the automobile – or spin-off new products themselves – the smart phone in the case of the computer – then the additional employment gains from the new technologies can offset any employment losses. One Post-Keynesian economist summarizes the possible results of technological unemployment as follows:

> Understandably enough, the redundant workers may create serious problems of adaptation, yet they have become redundant. Society as a whole can obtain the same quantities of goods as before without their "toil and trouble." The solution of these difficulties clearly cannot be that of preventing the introduction of the machines, as the "Luddite" workers thought in the nineteenth century. This would mean arresting the application of technical progress.... The correct answer to the problem is clearly that of introducing the machines, of producing with them the same physical quantities as before with fewer workers, and of employing the workers that have become redundant in the production of other commodities, old and new. Or, alternatively, to increase for all the proportion of leisure time to total time. (Pasinetti 1981, 231)

So, while a path to re-employment is identified by Pasinetti, notice that he posits an alternative remedy to technological unemployment in the reduction of working time for all workers.

The US automobile industry in the 1940s and 1950s was confronting a similar situation. The autoworkers' union, the UAW, represented the majority of workers in auto assembly plants throughout the country. The union was strong and local plant managers faced challenges to attempts to speed up the assembly line. In 1949, conflict between labor and management reached a breaking point at one large Ford Motor plant in Detroit, and over 62,000 workers went on strike for more than three weeks. While small-scale experiments with automation – replacing semiskilled workers with machines – had previously taken place, as a result of the strike "the prospect of an almost workerless factory teased and tantalized Ford officials" (Meyer 2002, 69). So, in the early 1950s, Ford opened a new plant that relied heavily on automated production processes. The result was to create a plant that used fewer workers. In particular, automation shrank the number of mid-skilled jobs, so most workers were either low-skilled or highly skilled – a prelude to what the economy would experience decades later. The specter of technology-driven unemployment was on the minds of union officials at the annual meeting of the UAW in 1954 when the impact of automation in the workplace was described as threatening to "create a social and economic nightmare in which men walk idle and hungry, made obsolete as producers because the mechanical monsters around them cannot replace them as consumers" (Meyer 2002, 73). Throughout the 1950s, union workers began to call for the six-hour day as a practical policy to combat unemployment and equitably distribute the productivity gains brought about through the use of new technology. As one worker at the time argued, "We say: place the benefits of science and new invention at the service of the people. Let's have the 6-hour day – and get paid for 8" (Cutler 2014, 33).

Technology, Skills, Tasks and the Transformation of Work

In the auto example above, notice the uneven effects of technology on the work process. Older skilled auto manufacturing occupations were redefined. New combinations of skills were needed to set up and operate the automated equipment. So while some workers were made redundant, other skilled jobs were being created. This is an early example of what mainstream economists refer to as skill-biased technological change. New technology creates the need for complementary skills and workers who can adapt to the new methods of production. Simultaneously, the technology reduces the demand for workers whose jobs are now outsourced to machines. This process repeated itself throughout the 1960s and 1970s in manufacturing plants that adopted numerically controlled (NC) machines. This reduced the need for highly skilled machinists in favor of less-skilled machine operators together with white-collar engineers and managers (Noble 1984, 238–9). These changes, resulting in the reduction of shop-floor workers' skills, wages, bargaining power and control over the pace of production, did not go unchallenged. In the case of the auto industry, toolmakers were traditionally assigned the job of setting up, adjusting, preparing and programming machinery to produce new parts. These workers, through their union representatives, argued that they should be assigned the job of programmer instead of giving that job title to the industrial engineers. The dispute was presented to an outside umpire or arbitrator whose decision sided with the toolmakers (Noble 1984, 254–5). This example illustrates that both the introduction and implementation of new technology is often contested and contingent. This example illustrates the political economy viewpoint that the adoption of new technology is not a pre-determined outcome. It lies in contrast to the idea – labeled technological determinism – that technological change is inevitable and that new technologies, if adopted, must therefore be more efficient and more productive.

Take the case of computer software packages replete with word processing, spreadsheet and presentation capabilities. Between four and five decades ago, the term "word processing" was meant to describe a centralized corporate department on a par with the more common data processing unit. The goal in creating these departments was to reduce the number of personal secretaries tasked with filing, answering phones and typing. For example, if typing could be undertaken in a central office with specialized typists (word processors), productivity would soar. Note that this was likely to both reduce the employment of secretaries and deskill the clerical workforce since, unlike the word processors who replaced them, secretaries deployed a wide variety of physical, cognitive and social interactive skills (Glenn and Feldberg 1977). The desktop computer, together with specialized software, took the routine tasks of typing, tabulating and organizing information and automated them, to an extent. The machines still needed to be activated and controlled by human workers. But the trend, according to Braverman, was to deskill the office workforce by removing control, judgment and decision-making from the individual worker so they became "so many mechanical eyes, fingers and voices whose functioning is, insofar as possible, predetermined by both rules and machinery" (1974, 340). The deskilled office worker would also receive a lower wage. Interpreted through the lens of class conflict and power, the use of office technology undercut the discretion and control of office workers, removed skill from their jobs and therefore allowed employers to pay them a lower wage.

To the extent that the new office technology took the form of computers and computer software, mainstream economists explained its effects on workers through the theory of skill-biased technical change. For proponents of the theory, jobs that primarily involve working with computer technology will be characterized by rising wages and employment gains relative to other occupations. Some of the computer activities associated with higher wages include the use of word processing and spreadsheets as well as e-mail. Workers whose skills complement the new technology will benefit. So there is a bias toward workers who are able to utilize these skills in the performance of new tasks. In addition, according to this theory, more highly educated workers were more likely to use computers and so the well-known human capital relationship between education and earnings was partially attributed to the use of computers (Krueger 1993). The skill-biased technical change argument quickly became the leading mainstream neoclassical explanation for rising wage inequality in the 1980s and 1990s. The message was simple: workers who acquire education and the skills compatible with computer technology will thrive, and those who do not will be left behind. Education then became the primary policy advanced to solve the income inequality problem.

But how would the story of computers in the workplace change if we reversed the line of reasoning so that higher-wage workers were more likely to use computers than other workers? That was the question posed by the authors of a study looking at German workers. Since white-collar and blue-collar workers use different technology, the economic advantage – higher wages – of using computers was really an advantage of being a white-collar worker. They tested this explanation by examining the economic return to using pencils. They found that jobs that require pencils also saw a wage boost. It is difficult to imagine pencils as particularly skill-enhancing tools for twentieth-century work. So, instead of computers leading to high wages, it might be that jobs that require the use of pencils and computers – white-collar jobs – pay higher wages. This would be even more likely if it was found that jobs requiring the use of hand tools (hammers, for example) paid less, and the study found this to be the case. The effect might not be determined by the tool but rather the location of the job in the wage hierarchy (DiNardo and Pischke 1997). Furthermore, skill-biased technical change theory focused on high-skill, high-wage jobs. It was not able to explain the more recent trend toward job polarization: growth in both low-skill/low-wage jobs and high-skill/high-wage jobs, together with declining middle-wage jobs.

So, in response, an alternative political economy interpretation of these findings argues that the rising return to white-collar work is connected to the long-term shift in economic power away from unionized, production and manufacturing jobs and toward managers, finance-sector professionals and administrative support workers. For example, one Marxist explanation rests on the identification of many white-collar jobs in management as unproductive, meaning that they do not add to the production of value but are a drain on profits (Moseley 1997). Recall that managers are charged with maintaining control over the workforce. Furthermore, according to the Marxist approach, the organization of production that is selected is the one that complements managerial control even when more efficient options (e.g. worker cooperatives) are available. Management's goal is to get workers to contribute work effort over and above that which is necessary to cover their wages. If successful, this enables profits – the source of management income – to grow. Also note that some white-collar workers are tasked with moving commodities more rapidly from production to final sale by creating demand for products through advertising and marketing. These supervisors and white-collar workers do not create value but they do enforce the power of capital on the shop floor and, once produced, assist in its circulation through the market (Mohoun 2014).

More recently, mainstream economists have explored not only the jobs affected by technological change but also the sets of tasks that comprise those jobs. For example, tasks can be broken down into two types: routine and non-routine. Routine tasks are those that follow rule-based commands (Levy and Murnane 2005). They may involve physical or manual routines (e.g. moving containers in a warehouse), cognitive tasks (e.g. counting how many items are on the warehouse shelves) or combinations of manual and cognitive tasks. For example, Wal-Mart is introducing robots in its stores. The robots will travel down the store aisles to determine what products need to be re-stocked, and which items are misplaced or mispriced. The robots communicate the information to human staff who will replenish, replace and re-price items. The robots are 50 percent faster than humans and they make fewer mistakes. The company reports that it will not reduce staff as a result (Bose 2017). That may be partly because the task of sorting, picking and stocking items is not yet feasible for robots. Similarly, in Amazon's warehouses, robots are increasingly being used to transport huge bins of products across the warehouse floor to workers who need to sort and package them. This has created two tiers of employment: one tier for skilled workers who can charge, track and maintain the robots, and a lower-paid tier of workers who perform manual labor once they receive a load of products from the robot (Kitroeff 2016). However, each year these corporations make more progress in automating the lower-tier jobs, so each year stock clerks and warehouse workers become more and more vulnerable to unemployment (Morris 2017).

To summarize, using task-based categories, jobs can be classified as: (1) routine manual, (2) routine cognitive, (3) non-routine manual and (4) non-routine cognitive tasks

– with (1) and (2) being most susceptible to automation. Jobs classified as non-routine require adaptability and flexibility in the face of unscripted situations, and are much more difficult to automate. Non-routine jobs are most commonly found in both high-wage and low-wage occupations. This classification scheme has been used to empirically estimate the relationship between employment growth and occupational income (Autor 2010; Acemoglu and Autor 2011). One political economy-based critique of this approach disputes the identification of low-wage with low-skill, and high-wage with high-skill. In particular, the non-routine task category fails to adequately distinguish between low-wage interactive service jobs and professional, managerial jobs. Both involve non-routine tasks. But service jobs such as those found in retail, food and personal services, along with child and elder care, are labeled "manual" jobs, whereas professional and managerial non-routine jobs are described as "cognitive." This distinction stems largely from the wage rather than from the nature of the tasks performed. Think for a moment about the hair stylist – a low-wage service provider – who requires knowledge about the physical characteristics of the client's hair, the effect of chemical treatments on that particular hair type, the emotional state of the customer, and alternatives and solutions to problems that arise and need to be implemented within a fixed block of scheduled time. This job is categorized as manual non-routine requiring few cognitive skills. Yet in one empirical analysis of the wage premium (higher wage) or penalty (lower wage) associated with occupational tasks, it was found that in low-wage jobs for which critical thinking, problem solving and other cognitive skills were important, workers received a wage premium. Since this premium was reported for both low-wage as well as high-wage workers, it is a mistake to unilaterally label low-wage workers as low-skilled. On the other hand, low-wage workers in occupations for which non-routine skills such as interpersonal, communicative skills were important received a wage penalty. By contrast, high-wage jobs in which interpersonal skills were an important part of the job did not suffer a wage penalty (Pietrykowski 2017a). So, from the political economy perspective, low-wage workers are not necessarily low-skill, and their non-routine interactive and communicative skills are undervalued in the labor market.

Another criticism of the mainstream neoclassical model that also shifts the focus to low-wage workers comes from feminist political economy. Almost everyone agrees that technological change is incompatible with jobs requiring caring labor (e.g. child care, teaching, health care and social work). Furthermore, the number of these jobs is growing. Care work can be found in both low-wage and high-wage occupations. So a missing part of the technological change story is the growing role of caring labor in the economy. This labor is often most likely to be performed by women. As such, it often carries a wage penalty due to the devaluation of the skills associated with women's work (Dwyer 2013). The question that remains is how impervious non-routine jobs are to automation. And, furthermore, how much of a threat is large-scale automation to work as we know it?

Automation and Robots in the Workplace

Do robots, artificial intelligence and machine learning represent a set of technologies that will transform the workplace? The pace and scope of change in this "digital revolution" have caused some to argue that the specter of large-scale technological unemployment is nearly upon us (Brynjolfsson and McAfee 2011). For instance, the job of "data conversion operator" reached its peak employment in the United States in 1997. The postal service used these workers to decipher addresses that machines could not read. The skills required knowledge of geography, languages and intuitive problem-solving. However, with improvements in handwriting character recognition these jobs could be automated (Nixon 2013). In fact, even traditionally high-wage professions requiring extensive years of education and training are increasingly subject to automation. Take the case of medical doctors. Diagnostic tools in the form of computers are able to take patient information and, when combined with tests and reviews of the latest medical literature, arrive at treatment options that are often more effective than those provided by flesh-and-blood physicians. Given the brief time doctors interact with patients, they are susceptible to "anchoring bias," whereby one or two symptoms fix the doctor's attention at the expense of multiple other conditions and symptoms. Now, while a robot doctor is still in the future, the use of computers in training, advising and support to far-flung patients in under-served parts of the world is a real likelihood that will end up re-structuring primary health care occupations (Cohn 2013).

Rather than examining the tasks most likely to be automated, one study analyzed the task content of jobs that have been traditionally cited as most resistant to automation (Frey and Osborne 2017). Three sets of tasks were identified as challenges to computer automation: (1) perception and manipulation; (2) creative intelligence; and (3) social intelligence. Perception and manipulation are characterized by dexterity and physical coordination. Creative intelligence is associated with artistic skill and aesthetic sensibilities. Finally, social intelligence is the ability to persuade, negotiate and accurately interpret the behavior and emotions of others. Not surprisingly, category (1) tasks were identified as having a high risk of computerization. Categories (2) and (3) were found to have a relatively lower risk. Overall, however, it was found that nearly 50 percent of 700 occupations analyzed had a high risk of computer automation. Another study, this one focusing just on industrial robots, estimated that between three and six workers will lose their jobs for every one additional robot. Wages, in turn, will decline between 0.25 and 0.5 percent (Acemoglu and Restrepo 2017). The study took into account the compensatory factors associated with lower prices for robot-produced goods and higher productivity in the economy overall. Currently, the total cost of operating a programmable robot, including the cost of training a worker to maintain the robot, could be recouped after only one year of operation when compared to the cost of employing the equivalent of two full-time workers each working one shift per day.[1]

As the example of the auto industry in the 1950s illustrated, automation itself is not a new phenomenon. When we zoom out to consider information technology, computers and software programs as types of automation that exist alongside robots, the employment-dampening effects are less apparent. So, another side of the political economy debate on technical change looks at the legacy of labor and technology as one in which the control over the introduction and use of new machines and automated processes looms large. For workers represented by industrial unions, it is the industry rather than the occupation that matters when discussing the effects of new technology. So, from this perspective, the attention on robots and automation misses the primary causes of wage stagnation and employment declines. Instead we should look to globalization, off-shoring of production to low-wage countries, and anti-union and neoliberal free-market labor policies (Mishel and Bivens 2017).

Recall that we began our discussion of work by exploring the unique feature of labor and the distinction between animal workers and human workers. We return to this issue now by pointing out that the European Parliament was asked to consider the establishment of a category of "legal personhood" for advanced robots. This would give them "specific rights and obligations, including that of making good any damage they may cause, and applying electronic personality to cases where robots make smart autonomous decisions or otherwise interact with third parties independently" (Delvaux 2017, 12).

The story of robots is not a simple one and their full impacts are diverse and still largely unknown. Robots are competitors and co-workers. They can make our lives easier and comfortable or more uncertain and precarious. As the report to the EU Parliament notes (see Text box 6.1), there are both beneficial and harmful effects of automation on economies and societies. For instance, robots and automated machines perform tasks that are dangerous and harmful to human health – for example, robots located spent nuclear fuel rods after the Fukushima nuclear plant meltdown (Fackler 2017). Automation has also lowered the incidence of occupational injury in assembly-line work requiring the lifting and handling of heavy parts and equipment. But the possibility of a future workplace in which robots are our co-workers, machine learning transforms professional white-collar tasks into easily programmable and adaptable algorithms, and the jobs displaced by technology outnumber the new jobs created by machines cannot be ignored. In one study (Felton, Raj and

Text box 6.1 European Parliament Report on the Social and Economic Impact of Robots

In 2015, the European Parliament's Committee on Legal Affairs drafted a report for the Commission on Civil Law Rules on Robotics. Its assessment of the impact of robots, artificial intelligence and machine learning included the following formal declarations:

- Now that humankind stands on the threshold of an era when ever more sophisticated robots, bots, androids and other manifestations of artificial intelligence ("AI") seem to be poised to unleash a new industrial revolution, which is likely to leave no stratum of society untouched, it is vitally important for the legislature to consider its legal and ethical implications and effects, without stifling innovation;
- Over the past 200 years employment figures had persistently increased due to the technological development; whereas the development of robotics and AI may have the potential to transform lives and work practices, raise efficiency, savings, and safety levels, provide enhanced level of services in the short to medium term robotics and AI promise to bring benefits of efficiency and savings, not only in production and commerce, but also in areas such as transport, medical care, rescue, education and farming, while making it possible to avoid exposing humans to dangerous conditions, such as those faced when cleaning up toxically polluted sites;
- The development of robotics and AI may result in a large part of the work now done by humans being taken over by robots without fully replenishing the lost jobs, so raising concerns about the future of employment, the viability of social welfare and security systems and the continued lag in pension contributions, if the current basis of taxation is maintained, creating the potential for increased inequality in the distribution of wealth and influence, while, for the preservation of social cohesion and prosperity, the likelihood of levying tax on the work performed by a robot or a fee for using and maintaining a robot should be examined in the context of funding the support and retraining of unemployed workers whose jobs have been reduced or eliminated;
- In the face of increasing divisions in society, with a shrinking middle class, it is important to bear in mind that developing robotics may lead to a high concentration of wealth and influence in the hands of a minority. (Delvaux 2017)

Seamons 2017), the top ten jobs most likely to be impacted by artificial intelligence include those of airline pilots, surgeons, dentists, biochemists and physicists. This is one of the issues motivating political economists to envision a world beyond wage labor. Note that this need not entail a world without work. Rather, according to some Marxist, post-Marxist and feminist political economists, current attempts to create meaningful work and the struggle over the ownership and control of robots, computers and other means of production are worthy of serious investigation.

7
Conclusion: Future Worlds of Work

There are several possible worlds of work that we can envision. In the near term, work is not going to disappear. There remain jobs and tasks that seem impervious to automation. These are not exclusively, as it is commonly asserted, high-wage professional-sector jobs. For instance, it is increasingly the case that the tasks carried out by human resource managers and financial advisors can be undertaken by robots (Schechner 2017). But, at the other end of the wage scale, it is notoriously hard to automate the social perceptiveness and empathy required of service workers in restaurants, child care, personal service and health care settings. These jobs comprise the work of caring laborers whose skills are frequently undervalued. These individuals perform necessary tasks of social reproduction. Care work takes place in households (families) and institutions such as schools, elder care facilities and community centers. While some countries, notably Sweden, regulate care work and provide opportunities for professional development, in many other countries care workers often labor for low pay under poor working conditions. In the case of elder care, for example, there is a shift toward private provision of services within the home. A shortage of care workers in Europe and North America has meant that the workforce is increasingly comprised of economically vulnerable workers with few options for alternative means of employment.

One proposal for improving the work of low-wage service workers is to enact a social wage whereby both formal, market-based care workers and informal, unpaid care workers receive payments in consideration of the valuable social reproduction tasks they perform. This would require redefining the family wage away from the outmoded, patriarchal ideal enshrined in the concept of a male breadwinner and toward that of a family-sustaining income. The social wage would compensate for the depletion of social reproduction that occurs when the provision of care work exceeds the flows of resources (sleep, emotional support, material well-being) necessary to sustain it (Figart, Mutari and Power 2005; Simonazzi 2008; Rai, Hoskyns and Thomas 2014).

In addition, a social wage calls attention to the recognition of caring labor as that which cannot be confined within the category of wage labor. Consider unpaid care work provided in the home by (usually female) caregivers. This work involves a wide range of tasks and services including emotional, sexual and affective labor, the physical production of goods (e.g. meals) and services (e.g. clean clothes), and the production and reproduction of culture and community (e.g. cooking indigenous food, organizing ritual events) (Rai, Hoskyns and Thomas 2014). Sylvia Federici notes that:

> [T]he struggle of immigrant domestic workers fighting for the institutional recognition of "carework" is strategically very important, for the devaluation of reproductive work has been one of the pillars of capital accumulation and the capitalistic exploitation of women's labor. Forcing the state to pay a "social wage" or a "guaranteed income" guaranteeing our reproduction also remains a key political objective, as the state is holding hostage much of the wealth we have produced. In this way it begins to transform the meaning of the wage in a similar fashion to the wages for housework movement. (2012, 12)

Moving from the short to the medium term, even if there is an employment-creating effect from technological change, the ownership of technology and the economic profits resulting from that ownership will generally exacerbate patterns of income inequality. The distribution of income away from workers and toward owners of capital will dampen the demand for new goods and services produced by automation

(Acemoglu and Restrepo 2018). The social wage is not the only proposal that attempts to address the problem of deteriorating working conditions and declining employment opportunities. The universal basic income is an idea with a long and varied lineage. The idea is to provide all adult citizens with a minimum income, regardless of their work situation. Some political economists argue that such a program is necessary in order to deal with the job-displacing effect of automation (Reich 2016). This is not a new idea, having been perhaps most famously associated with the concept of a negative income tax proposed in the early 1960s by the conservative economist Milton Friedman. But to equate Friedman's negative income tax with universal basic income is somewhat misleading. Friedman's negative income tax provides a basic minimum income only until an individual's income from work reaches a certain level, at which the basic income would disappear. The idea was to gradually reduce the subsidy to working individuals in order to reduce the disincentive to work. So, in this way – and keeping with the conservative anti-statist ideas of Friedman – the negative income tax was created as a means to eliminate the welfare state (Moffitt 2003).

By contrast, a universal basic income is understood as a cash payment to every citizen, without work requirements or restrictions (Van Parijs 2004). It can be distributed at the level of the national, regional or local government jurisdiction. The funds could be obtained through income tax revenue, or taxes on profits, property or new technologies like robots and artificial intelligence. Experiments with universal basic income have been tried in the past and are currently experiencing a revival in Quebec, Finland, Brazil, India, Lesotho, Namibia and South Africa (Bardhan 2017; Healy, McNeill, Cameron and Gibson 2018). In a 2017 Finnish experiment, 2,000 unemployed individuals were selected to receive an additional sum on top of their unemployment benefits. Since it was restricted to the unemployed, it is not a universal income, and since payments do not provide enough money to live on it does not supplant the existing welfare support system. On the other hand, there is no requirement that individuals find a job and there is no reduction in benefits if they do return to employment. The percentage of part-time workers in Finland has steadily risen from 10 percent to over 14 percent from 2000 to 2016. So the payment scheme may act to stabilize income for those in part-time, precarious jobs (Henley 2017).

Debates within political economy over the feasibility of universal basic income rest on several competing claims and visions about the future of work. On the one hand, the income support could shield low-wage employers from paying their workers a living wage. Furthermore, if basic income payments substitute for a range of targeted programs aimed at food security and access to health care, they could weaken already-vulnerable welfare state programs. Finally, the focus on basic income, especially in response to the disappearance of work, distracts attention and resources that could be directed at immediate struggles to improve the wages and working conditions of currently employed workers (Sodha 2017).

Positioned on the other side of the debate are political economists who see in universal basic income a means to transition away from a system based on wage labor. From this vantage point, the interesting feature of a basic income program is its tendency to detach the receipt of income from the performance of wage labor while providing individuals and families with the means to develop their own capabilities and interests without being compelled to sell their labor (Wright 2006). Furthermore, universal basic income turns the work disincentive argument on its head. If workers are provided with an alternative source of income, they will be less inclined to take just any job they find. They would be able to better match a job to their own skills and interests and they would be better able to assess the quality of the working conditions when deciding where to work. The basic income would tend to shift the balance of power from capital to labor (Wright 2006). Finally, basic income generated through a redistribution of income and wealth produced through capitalist production could be redirected to the development of social production. By social production, political economists envision a system directed toward the satisfaction of human needs. Care work is a prime example of social production since it can be produced – perhaps more effectively – outside of the private market. As such, basic income, serving as a social wage, can help to overcome the devaluation of care work (Folbre and Nelson 2000).

This discussion begins to broaden the scope of activities that can count as work. The goal of creating opportunities for people to experience work that both provides for material needs and lends expression to people's creativity, sense of purpose and feelings of self-efficacy is a topic for continued research in political economy (Spencer 2014). It raises the question of whether meaningful work is compatible with wage labor under capitalism. Can all work under capitalism be rewarding and well paid? Is fulfilling, living-wage gig work or high-road employment possible for everyone? Or do we need to think about current ways to move beyond capitalist wage labor? These questions should help to frame future debates in the political economy of work.

The distribution of work today is increasingly uneven, with overwork for some individuals, particularly women working a double shift of paid work in the labor market and unpaid labor at home, and underwork for others (Weeks 2014). Focusing on paid labor, we find that the incidence of part-time work has been growing in most of the developed countries of the world over the course of the last quarter-century. In 2016, over 20 percent of the workforce was employed part-time in Great Britain, Germany, Japan, Denmark and the Netherlands.[1] Additionally, from 1970 to 2016, annual hours worked have declined substantially. Over that time period, French and Japanese workers, on average, worked 13 weeks less per year compared to US workers, who saw their hours of work fall by less than 3 weeks.[2] In spite of these differences, what these trends indicate is the diminishing role of paid labor in a growing number of people's lives. Nevertheless, for the majority of people in the world, paid labor remains a necessity. So, from the political economy perspective, demands for more work – full employment – and better work – higher wages, more benefits and improved working conditions – are priorities. However, what about the demand for less work as a way to re-balance the power of capital and labor? Both demands for shorter hours and for universal basic income are attempts to alter the terms upon which people negotiate their place in the world of work. In taking this turn toward less work, the possibilities to define a world of work outside of and beyond the capitalist labor market grow. As Weeks argues, "Basic income can be a demand to gain some measure of distance and separation from the wage relation, and that distance might in turn create the possibility of a life no longer so thoroughly and relentlessly dependent on work for its qualities" (2011, 145). For example, individuals possess a variety of skills and interests that do not map neatly onto the paid labor market. For instance, in a study of a low-income community in Detroit, Michigan, residents were surveyed about the type of work they could offer to their neighbors. In particular, they were asked to name the skills at which they were best, skills for which they could be hired and skills that they would like to teach others. The variety of responses that residents provided indicated that people differentiated between marketable skills and skills and interests that were valuable to the community (Pietrykowski 2015).

There is a growing interest in identifying the components of work beyond capitalism. For instance, the community economies perspective on the political economy of work tries to view the economy differently so that, instead of seeing work as primarily taking place in the capitalist labor market, work in the non-profit sector, in cooperatives, in voluntary associations, in civil society organizations, in neighborhoods, social networks and families becomes the center of attention (Gibson-Graham 1996). This process of de-centering the capitalist market exposes both the many ways of doing work and the particularity – and perhaps even the fragility and evanescence – of wage labor. In its place, new forms of work oriented toward meeting needs, involving relations of reciprocity and pro-social or other-regarding behavior, and an ethics of care are often, although not always, characteristic of these sites of work (Bowles 2016). Work in the future will still involve toil, strength, creativity and social interaction. But it may not involve wage labor that produces a surplus or profit for others. So the phrase "working for a living" will need to take on new meanings yet to be crafted.

Notes

1 Introduction: The Unique Character of Work

1 This account best describes the case of Britain, so it should be noted that feudalism morphed and declined at different rates in other nations. Brenner (1976) provides a rich account of the trajectory of feudalism across Europe.

2 For a brief summary of these debates, refer to Daniel Little's Understanding Society blog: http://understandingsociety. blogspot.com/2010/01/brenner-debate-revisited.html.

3 For a brief introduction to the current debate over the impact of slavery on capitalism, see Perry (2016).

4 Data sources for part-time workers: OECD, https://stats.oecd. org; and BLS, Current Population Survey, Labor Force Statistics: https://www.bls.gov/cps/#data.

5 Note that labor is a commodity in the sense that employers purchase the labor of workers for a period of time.

6 Note that these statistics are calculated from 2017 data representing the number of unemployed individuals including "discouraged workers" who have given up looking for work, part-time workers who seek full-time work, and those people available to work. Official unemployment statistics do not count these three categories of workers – Office of National Statistics: https://www.ons.gov.uk/economy/nationalaccounts/uksectoraccounts/articles/economicreview/october2017; Bureau of Labor Statistics, Alternative Measures of Labor Underutilization for States, 2017 Annual Averages: https://www.bls.gov/lau/stalt17q4.htm.

2 Inequality at Work: Skills, Wages and Productivity

1 This applies to post-secondary education where schooling is not mandated and individuals can choose whether or not to attend a college or technical school.
2 This is the median wage for plumbers in the United States according to the May 2016 Occupational Employment Statistics: https://www.bls.gov/oes/current/oes_nat.htm#49-0000.
3 Note that there are several variants of Marxist economic crisis theory, and the determinants of crisis are always influenced by specific economic and political conditions (Dunn 2011; Kotz 2015).

3 Gender at Work: Caring Labor

1 Examples include the American Time Use Survey (https://www.bls.gov/tus) and the Multinational Time Use Survey (https://www.timeuse.org/mtus).
2 The word "we" refers to Western cultures and the current 21st-century time period.
3 Still, it is important to take account of the social, political and cultural environment within which these communal alternatives to the private household exist. Some attempts to assert community control may inadvertently aid neoliberal regimes. For example, community kitchens begun in Bolivia and Peru in the 1980s were run by women leaders of the community as an extension of their status and power. As such, the existence of a community kitchen signaled the existence of entrepreneurial talent, which attracted development grants and projects. Equally important, the kitchens were staffed and managed by women's unpaid labor, thereby relieving the state from having to provide access to food for the community (Schroeder 2006).

4 Managerial Strategies: Low Road vs. High Road and Off-Road

1 Calculations by author based on OECD (2018).
2 Wage data obtained from www.upwork.com job website for iOS developer occupations.
3 https://support.taskrabbit.com/hc/en-us/articles/207555983-Am-I-a-TaskRabbit-employee.

5 Beyond Managerial Strategies: Worker Cooperatives

1 The websites associated with each of these projects are: (1) http://unsse.org (United Nations Social and Solidarity Economy); https://ussen.org (US Solidarity Economy); (2) www.communityeconomies.org (Community Economies); (3) www.parecon.org (Participatory Economics).

6 Technology, Automation and Skills: Restructuring the Workplace

1 Information obtained from Michael Folster, Robotics Product Manager, Behco-MRM, 5 March 2018.

7 Conclusion: Future Worlds of Work

1 OECD (2018), Part-time employment rate (indicator): https://data.oecd.org.
2 OECD (2018), Hours Worked: Average annual hours actually worked, OECD Employment and Labour Market Statistics (database), http://dx.doi.org/10.1787/data-00303-en; https://data.oecd.org.

References

Abad-Santos, A. (2013). Instead of Raises McDonald's Tells Workers to Sign Up for Food Stamps. *The Atlantic*: https://www.theatlantic.com/business/archive/2013/10/instead-living-wage-mcdonalds-tells-workers-sign-food-stamps.

Abbate, J. (2012). *Recoding Gender*. Cambridge University Press.

Acemoglu, D. and Autor, D. (2011). Skills, Tasks and Technologies. In O. Ashenefelter and D. Card, eds., *Handbook of Labor Economics* (Vol. IV). Amsterdam: Elsevier, pp. 1043–1171.

Acemoglu, D. and Restrepo, P. (2017). Robots and Jobs: Evidence from US Labor Markets (Working Paper No. w23285). National Bureau of Economic Research.

Acemoglu, D. and Restrepo, P. (2018). Artificial Intelligence, Automation and Work (Working Paper No. w24196). National Bureau of Economic Research.

Adelstein, J. (2017). Japan is Literally Working Itself to Death. *Forbes*: https://www.forbes.com/sites/adelsteinjake/2017/10/30/japan-is-literally-working-itself-to-death-how-can-it-stop.

Agarwal, B. (1997). Bargaining and Gender Relations: Within and Beyond the Household. *Feminist Economics*, 3(1): pp. 1–51.

Aglietta, M. (1979). *A Theory of Capitalist Regulation: The U.S. Experience*. New York: Verso.

Aguiar, L. L. M. (2016). Sweatshop Citizenship, Precariousness and Organizing Building Cleaners. In R. Lambert and A. Herod, eds., *Neoliberal Capitalism and Precarious Work*. Cheltenham, Glos.: Edward Elgar Publishing, pp. 255–76.

Albelda, R. P. (1986). Occupational Segregation by Race and Gender, 1958–1981. *ILR Review*, 39(3): pp. 404–11.

Alecop Group (n.d.). www.alecop.com/en/learning-services/work-study-learning-program.

Alkire, S. (2005). Why the Capability Approach? *Journal of Human Development*, 6(1): pp. 115–35.

Alonso-Villar, O. and Del Río, C. (2013). Occupational Segregation of Black Women in the United States: A Look at its Evolution from 1940 to 2010. (Working Paper ECINEQ WP2013-304). Society for the Study of Economic Inequality: www.ecineq.org/milano/WP/ECINEQ2013-304.pdf.

Altintas, E. and Sullivan, O. (2016). Fifty Years of Change Updated: Cross-national Gender Convergence in Housework. *Demographic Research*, 35: pp. 455–69.

Andersson, T., Kazemi, A., Tengblad, S. and Wickelgren, M. (2011). Not the Inevitable Bleak House? The Positive Experiences of Workers and Managers in Retail Work in Sweden. In I. Grugulis and O. Bozkurt, eds., *Retail Work*. Basingstoke: Palgrave Macmillan, pp. 253–76.

Applebaum, E., Bailey, T., Berg, P. and Kalleberg, A. (2000). *Manufacturing Advantage*. Ithaca: Cornell University Press.

Arando, S., Freundlich, F., Gago, M., Jones, D. C., Kato, T. and Carberry, E. C. (2011). Assessing Mondragon: Stability and Institutional Adaptation in the Face of Globalization. In E. J. Carberry, ed., *Employee Ownership and Shared Capitalism*. Champaign, IL: Labor and Employment Relations Association, pp. 241–71.

Arestis, P. (1996). Post-Keynesian Economics: Towards Coherence. *Cambridge Journal of Economics*, 20(1): pp. 111–35.

Ariely, D., Kamenica, E. and Prelec, D. (2008). Man's Search for Meaning: The Case of Legos. *Journal of Economic Behavior & Organization*, 67(3–4): pp. 671–7.

Autor, D. (2010). *The Polarization of Job Opportunities in the US Labor Market* [pdf]. Washington DC: Center for American Progress and The Hamilton Project: www.hamiltonproject.org/papers/the_polarization_of_job_opportunities_in_the_u.s._labor_market_implica.

Baptist, E. E. (2014). *The Half Has Never Been Told: Slavery and the Making of American Capitalism*. New York: Basic Books.

Bardhan, P. (2017). Universal Basic Income – Its Special Case for India. *Indian Journal of Human Development*, 11(2): pp. 141–3.

Bartley, S. J., Blanton, P. W. and Gilliard, J. L. (2005). Husbands and Wives in Dual-Earner Marriages. *Marriage & Family Review*, 37(4): pp. 69–94.

Batt, R., Lee, J. E. and Lakhani, T. (2014). High Road 2.0: A National Study of Human Resource Practices, Turnover, and Customer Service in the Restaurant Industry. New York: ROC United, pp. 1–32: http://rocunited.org/publications/a-national-study-of-human-resource-practices-turnover-and-customer-service-in-the-restaurant-industry.

Becker, G. S. (1962). Investment in Human Capital. *Journal of Political Economy*, 70(5, Part 2): pp. 9–49.

Becker, Gary S. (1981). *A Treatise on the Family*. Cambridge, MA: Harvard University Press.

Beckert, S. (2015). *Empire of Cotton*. New York: Vintage Press.

Bertrand, M. and Mullainathan, S. (2004). Are Emily and Greg More Employable than Lakisha and Jamal? A Field Experiment on Labor Market Discrimination. *American Economic Review*, 94(4): pp. 991–1013.

Bhaduri, A. and Marglin, S. (1990). Unemployment and the Real Wage: The Economic Basis for Contesting Political Ideologies. *Cambridge Journal of Economics*, 14(4): pp. 375–93.

Bittman, M., England, P., Sayer, L., Folbre, N. and Matheson, G. (2003). When Does Gender Trump Money? Bargaining and Time in Household Work. *American Journal of Sociology*, 109(1): pp. 186–214.

Bivens, J. and Mishel, L. (2013). The Pay of Corporate Executives and Financial Professionals as Evidence of Rents in Top 1 Percent Incomes. *Journal of Economic Perspectives*, 27(3): pp. 57–78.

Blanding, M. and White, H. (2015). How China is Screwing Over its Poisoned Factory Workers. *Wired*: https://www.wired.com/2015/04/inside-chinese-factories.

Booth, R. (2018). DPD Courier Who Was Fined for Day Off Dies from Diabetes. *Guardian*: https://www.theguardian.com/business/2018/feb/05/courier-who-was-fined-for-day-off-to-see-doctor-dies-from-diabetes.

Bose, N. (2017). Wal-Mart's New Robots Scan Shelves to Re-Stock Items Faster. *Reuters*: https://www.reuters.com/article/us-usa-walmart-robots/wal-marts-new-robots-scan-shelves-to-restock-items-faster-idUSKBN1CV1N4.

Bowe, J., Bowe, M. and Streeter, R. (2000). *Gig*. New York: Crown Publishers.

Bowles, S. (1985). The Production Process in a Competitive Economy. *American Economic Review*, 75(1): pp. 16–36.

Bowles, S. (1998). Endogenous Preferences: The Cultural Consequences of Markets and Other Economic Institutions. *Journal of Economic Literature*, 36(1): pp. 75–111.

Bowles, S. (2016). *The Moral Economy: Why Good Incentives Are No Substitute for Good Citizens*. New Haven: Yale University Press.

Bowles, S. and Gintis, H. (1976). *Schooling in Capitalist America*. New York: Basic Books.

Bowles, S., Gintis, H. and Osborne, M. (2001a). Incentive-enhancing Preferences: Personality, Behavior, and Earnings. *American Economic Review*, 91(2): pp. 155–8.

Bowles, S., Gintis, H. and Osborne, M. (2001b). The Determinants of Earnings: A Behavioral Approach. *Journal of Economic Literature*, 39(4): pp. 1137–76.

Bowles, S., Gintis, H. and Osborne, M. (2008). Introduction. In S. Bowles, H. Gintis and M. Osborne, eds., *Unequal Chances: Family Background and Economic Success*. Princeton University Press, pp. 1–22.

Braverman, H. (1974). *Labor and Monopoly Capital*. New York: Monthly Review Press.

Brenner, R. (1976). Agrarian Class Structure and Economic Development in Pre-Industrial Europe. *Past & Present*, (70): pp. 30–75.

Brenner, R. (1977). The Origins of Capitalist Development. *New Left Review*, (104): pp. 25–92.

Brown, S. and Getz, C. (2008). Towards Domestic Fair Trade? *GeoJournal*, 73(1): pp. 11–22.

Brynjolfsson, E. and McAfee, A. (2011). *Race Against the Machine*. Lexington, MA: Digital Frontier Press.

Budig, M. J. and Misra, J. (2010). How Care-Work Employment Shapes Earnings in Cross-National Perspective. *International Labour Review*, 149(4): pp. 441–60.

Burawoy, M. (1979). *Manufacturing Consent*. University of Chicago Press.

Burdin, G. and Dean, A. (2009). New Evidence on Wages and Employment in Worker Cooperatives Compared with Capitalist Firms. *Journal of Comparative Economics*, 37(4): pp. 517–33.

Butler, P., Glover, L. and Tregaskis, O. (2011). "When the Going Gets Tough" … : Recession and the Resilience of Workplace Partnership. *British Journal of Industrial Relations*, 49(4): pp. 666–87.

Carvalho, L. and Rezai, A. (2015). Personal Income Inequality and Aggregate Demand. *Cambridge Journal of Economics*, 40(2): pp. 491–505.

Chan, J. (2013). A Suicide Survivor: Life of a Chinese Worker. *New Technology, Work and Employment*, 28(2): pp. 84–99.

Chan, J. and Pun, N. (2010). Suicide as Protest for the New Generation of Chinese Migrant Workers. *Asia-Pacific Journal: Japan Focus*, 8(37, 2): pp. 1–33.

Chantavanich, S., Laodumrongchai, S. and Stringer, C. (2016). Under the Shadow: Forced Labour among Sea Fishers in Thailand. *Marine Policy*, 68: pp. 1–7.

Chaudhuri, S. and Brown, E. (2017). IKEA Jumps into "Gig Economy" with Deal for TaskRabbit. *Wall Street Journal*: https://

www.wsj.com/articles/ikea-to-acquire-online-freelancer-market-place-taskrabbit-1506618421.

China Labor Watch (2016). Apple Making Big Profits but Chinese Workers' Wage on the Slide: www.chinalaborwatch.org/upfile/2016_08_23/Pegatron-report%20FlAug.pdf.

China Labor Watch and The Future in Our Hands (2015). Something's Not Right Here: http://digitalcommons.ilr.cornell.edu. proxy.lib.umich.edu/cgi/viewcontent.cgi?article=3963&context=globaldocs.

Clark, G. (2007). *A Farewell to Alms: A Brief Economic History of the World*. Princeton University Press.

Clegg, J. (2015). Capitalism and Slavery. *Critical Historical Studies*, 2(2): pp. 281–304.

Cohen, R. (2016). What Programming's Past Reveals about Today's Gender-Pay Gap. *The Atlantic*: https://www.theatlantic.com/business/archive/2016/09/what-programmings-past-reveals-about-todays-gender-pay-gap/498797.

Cohn, J. (2013). The Robot Will See You Now. *The Atlantic*: https://www.theatlantic.com/magazine/archive/2013/03/the-robot-will-see-you-now/309216.

Cooper, D. and Kroeger, T. (2017). *Employers Steal Billions from Workers' Paychecks Each Year*. Washington: Economic Policy Institute: www.epi.org/publication/employers-steal-billions-from-workers-paychecks-each-year-survey-data-show-millions-of-workers-are-paid-less-than-the-minimum-wage-at-significant-cost-to-taxpayers-and-state-economies.

Coppens, A. D., Alcalá, L., Mejía-Arauz, R. and Rogoff, B. (2014). Children's Initiative in Family Household Work in Mexico. *Human Development*, 57(2–3): pp. 116–30.

Craig, B. and Pencavel, J. (1992). The Behavior of Worker Cooperatives. *American Economic Review*, 82(5): pp. 1083–1105.

Cutler, J (2014). *Labor's Time: Shorter Hours, the UAW, and the Struggle for American Unionism*. Philadelphia: Temple University Press.

Dellheim, C. (1987). The Creation of a Company Culture: Cadburys, 1861–1931. *American Historical Review*, 92(1): pp. 13–44.

Delvaux, M. (2017). Motion for a European Parliament Resolution. PR\1095387EN.doc: www.europarl.europa.eu/sides/getDoc.do?pubRef=-//EP//TEXT+REPORT+A8-2017-0005+0+DOC+XML+V0//EN.

DiNardo, J. E. and Pischke, J. S. (1997). The Returns to Computer Use Revisited: Have Pencils Changed the Wage Structure Too? *Quarterly Journal of Economics*, 112(1): pp. 291–303.

Domar, E. D. (1962). On Total Productivity and All That. *Journal of Political Economy*, 70(6): pp. 597–608.

Dong, X. Y. and An, X. (2015). Gender Patterns and Value of Unpaid Care Work: Findings from China's First Large-Scale Time Use Survey. *Review of Income and Wealth*, 61(3): pp. 540–60.

Duffy, M. (2007). Doing the Dirty Work: Gender, Race, and Reproductive Labor in Historical Perspective. *Gender & Society*, 21(3): pp. 313–36.

Dunn, B. (2011). Marxist Crisis Theory and the Need to Explain Both Sides of Capitalism's Cyclicity. *Rethinking Marxism*, 23(4): pp. 524–42.

Dwyer, R. E. (2013). The Care Economy? Gender, Economic Restructuring and Job Polarization in the U.S. Labor Market. *American Sociological Review*, 78(3): pp. 390–416.

Edmonds, E. V. (2006). Understanding Sibling Differences in Child Labor. *Journal of Population Economics*, 19(4): pp. 795–821.

Edwards, R. (1979). *Contested Terrain*. New York: Basic Books.

Ellerman, D. (1990). *The Democratic Worker-owned Firm*. Boston: Unwin Hyman.

England, P. (1992). *Comparable Worth*. New York: Aldine de Gruyter.

England, P. (2010). The Gender Revolution: Uneven and Stalled. *Gender and Society*, 24(2): pp. 149–66.

England, P., Allison, P. and Wu, Y. (2007). Does Bad Pay Cause Occupations to Feminize, Does Feminization Reduce Pay, and How Can We Tell with Longitudinal Data? *Social Science Research*, 36(3): pp. 1237–56.

England, P., Budig, M. and Folbre, N. (2002). Wages of Virtue. *Social Problems*, 49(4): pp. 455–73.

English-Lueck, J. A. and Avery, M. L. (2017). Intensifying Work and Chasing Innovation. *Anthropology of Work Review*, 38(1): pp. 40–9.

Ensmenger, N. (2010). Making Programming Masculine. In T. Misa, ed., *Gender Codes*. New York: Wiley – IEEE Computer Society Press, pp. 115–41.

Fabricant, S. (1959). *The Study of Economic Growth*. Cambridge, MA: National Bureau of Economic Research.

Fackler, M. (2017). Six Years after Fukushima Robots Finally Find Reactors Melted Uranium Fuel. *New York Times* [online], p. D1: https://www.nytimes.com/2017/11/19/science/japan-fukushima-nuclear-meltdown-fuel.html.

Federici, S. (2012). *Revolution at Point Zero*. Oakland, CA: PM Press.

Felton, E. W., Raj, M. and Seamons, R. (2017). Linking Advances in Artificial Intelligence to Skills, Occupations, and Industries. In Allied Social Sciences Association Conference Preliminary

Program: https://www.aeaweb.org/conference/2018/preliminary/paper/EFD8kAG9.

Ferrant, G., Pesando, L. M. and Nowacka, K. (2014). Unpaid Care Work: The Missing Link in the Analysis of Gender Gaps in Labour Outcomes. *Centro de Desarrollo de la OCDE*, 5: pp. 1–12.

Figart, D. M., Mutari, E. and Power, M. (2005). *Living Wages, Equal Wages*. London: Routledge.

Folbre, N. and Nelson, J. (2000). For Love or Money – or Both? *Journal of Economic Perspectives*, 14(4): pp. 123–40.

Folbre, N. and Smith, K. (2017). The Wages of Care. Washington Center for Equitable Growth: http://equitablegrowth.org/working-papers/the-wages-of-care.

Ford, H. (1926). Mass Production. In *The Encyclopedia Britannica*, 13th edn. New York: The Encyclopedia Britannica, Inc., pp. 321–3.

Freeman, R. and Medoff, J. (1984). *What Do Unions Do?* New York: Basic Books.

Frey, C. B. and Osborne, M. A. (2017). The Future of Employment: How Susceptible are Jobs to Computerisation? *Technological Forecasting and Social Change*, 114: pp. 254–80.

Funari, C. (2018). New Belgium Cuts 4 Percent of Workforce Amid Craft Beer Slowdown. *Brewbound*: https://www.brewbound.com/news/new-belgium-cuts-4-percent-workforce-amid-craft-beer-slowdown.

Gibson-Graham, J. K. (1996). *The End of Capitalism (As We Knew It)*. Cambridge, MA and Oxford: Blackwell Publishers.

Gilman, C. P. (1998). *Women and Economics*. Berkeley: University of California Press: https://publishing.cdlib.org/ucpressebooks/view?docId=ft896nb5rd;brand=ucpress.

Gintis, H. (1989). Financial Markets and the Democratic Enterprise. In R. Drago and R. Perlman, eds., *Microeconomic Issues in Labour Economics: New Approaches*. New York: Harvester-Wheatsheaf, pp. 155–76.

Glenn, E. N. (1992). From Servitude to Service Work: Historical Continuities in the Racial Division of Paid Reproductive Labor. *Signs: Journal of Women in Culture and Society*, 18(1): pp. 1–43.

Glenn, E. N. (2012). *Forced to Care*. Cambridge, MA: Harvard University Press.

Glenn, E. N. and Feldberg, R. L (1977). Degraded and Deskilled: The Proletarianization of Clerical Work. *Social Problems*, 25(1): pp. 52–64.

Goldberg, A. E. (2013). "Doing" and "Undoing" Gender: The Meaning and Division of Housework in Same-Sex Couples. *Journal of Family Theory Review*, 5(2): pp. 85–104.

Goodman, P. S. and Soble, J. (2017). Global Economy's Stubborn Reality: Plenty of Work, Not Enough Pay. *New York Times*: https://www.nytimes.com/2017/10/07/business/unemployment-wages-economy.html?partner=bloomberg.

Gordon, D. M., Edwards, R. and Reich, M. (1982). *Segmented Work, Divided Workers*. Cambridge University Press.

Greene, A. N. (2008). *Horses at Work: Harnessing Power in Industrial America*. Cambridge, MA: Harvard University Press.

Gregg, M. (2011). *Work's Intimacy*. Cambridge: Polity.

Gunn, C. (2011). Workers' Participation in Management, Workers' Control of Production. *Review of Radical Political Economics*, 43(3): pp. 317–27.

Guy, M. E. and Newman, M. A. (2004). Women's Jobs, Men's Jobs: Sex Segregation and Emotional Labor. *Public Administration Review*, 64(3): pp. 289–98.

Hall, P. and Soskice, D. (2001). *Varieties of Capitalism*. Oxford University Press.

Hamermesh, D. S. and Biddle, J. E. (1994). Beauty and the Labor Market. *American Economic Review*, 84(5): pp. 1174–94.

Haraway, D. J. (2007). *When Species Meet*. Minneapolis: University of Minnesota Press.

Hardoon, D. (2017). An Economy for the 99% [pdf]. Oxford: Oxfam: https://policy-practice.oxfam.org.uk/publications/an-economy-for-the-99-its-time-to-build-a-human-economy-that-benefits-everyone-620170.

Harper, B. (2000). Beauty, Stature and the Labour Market. *Oxford Bulletin of Economics and Statistics*, 62(s1): pp. 771–800.

Hayden, D. (1981). *The Grand Domestic Revolution*. Cambridge, MA: MIT Press.

Healy, S., McNeill, J., Cameron, J. and Gibson, K. (2018). Pre-empting Apocalypse? Postcapitalism as an Everyday Politics. *AQ-Australian Quarterly*, 89(2): pp. 28–33.

Henley, J. (2017). Money for Nothing: Is Finland's Universal Basic Income Trial too Good to Be True? *Guardian*: https://www.theguardian.com/inequality/2018/jan/12/money-for-nothing-is-finlands-universal-basic-income-trial-too-good-to-be-true.

Heron, B. (1980). The Crisis of the Craftsman. *Labour / Le Travailleur*, 6: pp. 7–48.

Hertz, T. (2008). Rags, Riches and Race: The Intergenerational Economic Mobility of Black and White Families in the United States. In S. Bowles, H. Gintis and M. Osborne, eds., *Unequal Chances: Family Background and Economic Success*. Princeton University Press, pp. 165–91.

Hirsch, B. T. and Macpherson, D. A. (n.d.). www.unionstats.com.

Hobsbawm, E. (1964). *Labouring Men*. London: Weidenfeld and Nicolson.

Hochschild, A. R. (1983). *The Managed Heart*. Berkeley: University of California Press.

Holden, L. and Biddle, J. (2017). The Introduction of Human Capital Theory into Education Policy in the United States. *History of Political Economy*, 49(4): pp. 537–74.

Holyoake, G. J. (1893). *Self-help by the People: The History of the Rochdale Pioneers*. London: Swan Sonnenschein.

Horn, J. (2012). "A Beautiful Madness": Privilege, the Machine Question and Industrial Development in Normandy in 1789. *Past & Present*, 217(1): pp. 149–85.

Hounshell, D. (1984). *From American System to Mass Production, 1800–1932*. Baltimore: Johns Hopkins University Press.

Hribal, J. (2003). "Animals Are Part of the Working Class": A Challenge to Labor History. *Labor History*, 44(4): pp. 435–53.

Hudson, K. (2007). The New Labor Market Segmentation. *Social Science Research*, 36(1): pp. 286–312.

Humphries, J. (1990). Enclosures, Common Rights, and Women. *Journal of Economic History*, 50(1): pp. 17–42.

International Service System (2016). Group Annual Report: www.annualreport.issworld.com/2016.

Jacoby, S. (1997). *Modern Manors: Welfare Capitalism since the New Deal*. Princeton University Press.

Jarvis, H. (2013). Against the "Tyranny" of Single-Family Dwelling: Insights from Christiania at 40. *Gender, Place & Culture*, 20(8): pp. 939–59.

Jenkins, J. (2007). Gambling Partners? The Risky Outcomes of Workplace Partnerships. *Work, Employment and Society*, 21(4): pp. 635–52.

Jessop, B. (1990). Regulation Theories in Retrospect and Prospect. *Economy and Society*, 19(2): pp. 153–216.

Jonna, R. J. and Foster, J. B. (2016). Marx's Theory of Working-Class Precariousness. *Monthly Review*, 67(11): https://monthlyreview.org/2016/04/01/marxs-theory-of-working-class-precariousness.

Jossa, B. (2005). Marx, Marxism and the Cooperative Movement. *Cambridge Journal of Economics*, 29(1): pp. 3–18.

Kabeer, N. (2005). Gender Equality and Women's Empowerment. *Gender & Development*, 13(1): pp. 13–24.

Kaldor, N. (1955). Alternative Theories of Distribution. *Review of Economic Studies*, 23(2): pp. 83–100.

Kalecki, M. (1943). Political Aspects of Full Employment. *Political Quarterly*, 14(4): pp. 322–30.

Kamano, S. (2009). Housework and Lesbian Couples in Japan. *Women's Studies International Forum*, 32(2): pp. 130–41.

Katz, H. and Darbishire, O. (2000). *Converging Divergences*. Ithaca: Cornell University Press.

Katz, J. (2015). How Nonemployed Americans Spend Their Weekdays: Men vs Women. *New York Times*: https://www.nytimes.com/interactive/2015/01/06/upshot/how-nonemployed-americans-spend-their-weekdays-men-vs-women.html.

Kaufman, B. E. (2001). The Theory and Practice of Strategic HRM and Participative Management. *Human Resource Management Review*, 11(4): pp. 505–33.

Kennedy, E. J. (2010). The Invisible Corner: Expanding Workplace Rights for Female Day Laborers. *Berkeley Journal of Employment and Labor Law*, 31: pp. 126–59.

Kilbourne, B. S., Farkas, G., Beron, K., Weir, D. and England, P. (1994). Returns to Skill, Compensating Differentials, and Gender Bias. *American Journal of Sociology*, 100(3): pp. 689–719.

Kitroeff, N. (2016). Warehouses Promised Lots of Jobs, but Robot Workforce Slows Hiring. *LA Times*: www.latimes.com/projects/la-fi-warehouse-robots.

Kochan, T. A., Katz, H. C. and McKersie, R. B. (1986). *The Transformation of American Industrial Relations*. Ithaca: Cornell University Press.

Kotz, D. M. (2015). Capitalism and Forms of Capitalism: Levels of Abstraction in Economic Crisis Theory. *Review of Radical Political Economics*, 47(4): pp. 541–9.

Krueger, Alan B. (1993). How Computers Have Changed the Wage Structure. *Quarterly Journal of Economics*, 108(1): pp. 33–60.

Landefeld, J. S. and McCulla, S. H. (2000). Accounting for Nonmarket Household Production within a National Accounts Framework. *Review of Income and Wealth*, 46(3): pp. 289–307.

Latinne, A. (2014). *The Mondragon Cooperatives*. Cambridge: Intersentia.

Lazonick, W. (1974). Karl Marx and Enclosures in England. *Review of Radical Political Economics*, 6(2): pp. 1–59.

Leidner, R. (1999). Emotional Labor in Service Work. *Annals of the American Academy of Political and Social Science*, 561(1): pp. 81–95.

Leung, P. (2015). *Labor Activists and the New Working Class in China*. New York: Palgrave Macmillan.

Levy, F. and Murnane, R. J. (2005). *The New Division of Labor: How Computers Are Creating the Next Job Market*. Princeton University Press.

Lewchuk, W. (1993). Men and Monotony: Fraternalism at the Ford Motor Company. *Journal of Economic History*, 53(4): pp. 1–30.

Lindsley, G. (2017). Working at Google Seemed Like a Dream Job. The Reality has been a Tedious, Pointless Nightmare. *Washington Post*: https://www.washingtonpost.com/news/posteverything/wp/2017/10/17/my-google-job-was-tedious-and-pointless/?utm_term=.a00baf5ec57a.

Lloyd, C. and Payne, J. (2006). Goodbye to All That? A Critical Re-evaluation of the Role of the High Performance Work Organization Within the UK Skills Debate. *Work, Employment and Society*, 20(1): pp. 151–65.

Locke, C. (2017). Meet the People Who Pick Up When You Call Customer Service. *Wired*: https://www.wired.com/2017/01/jose-sarmento-matos-how-can-i-help-you.

Lundberg, S. and Pollak, R. (1996). Bargaining and Distribution in Marriage. *Journal of Economic Perspectives*, 10(4): pp. 139–58.

Major, G. (1996). Solving the Underinvestment and Degeneration Problems of Workers' Cooperatives. *Annals of Public and Cooperative Economics*, 67(4): pp. 545–601.

Mandel, H. (2013). Up the Down Staircase: Women's Upward Mobility and the Wage Penalty for Occupational Feminization, 1970–2007. *Social Forces*, 91(4): pp. 1183–1207.

Manuel, F. E. (1938). The Luddite Movement in France. *Journal of Modern History*, 10(2): pp. 180–211.

Marglin, S. A. (1974). What Do Bosses Do? The Origins and Functions of Hierarchy in Capitalist Production. *Review of Radical Political Economics*, 6(2): pp. 60–112.

Marschke, M. and Vandergeest, P. (2016). Slavery Scandals: Unpacking Labour Challenges and Policy Responses within the Off-shore Fisheries Sector. *Marine Policy*, 68: pp. 39–46.

Marx, K. (1977). *Capital* (Vol. I). New York: Vintage.

Marx, K. (1887/2015). *Capital* (Vol. I). Marxists Internet Archive: https://www.marxists.org/archive/marx/works/download/pdf/Capital-Volume-I.pdf.

Mayer, G. (2004). *Union Membership Trends in the United States*. Washington, DC: Congressional Research Service.

McNally, D. (1990). *Political Economy and the Rise of Capitalism*. University of California Press.

Mellizo, P., Carpenter, J. and Matthews, P. H. (2017). Ceding Control: An Experimental Analysis of Participatory Management. *Journal of the Economic Science Association*, 3(1): pp. 62–74.

Meyer, S. (2002). "An Economic 'Frankenstein'": UAW Workers' Responses to Automation at the Ford Brook Park Plant in the 1950s. *Michigan Historical Review*, 28(1): pp. 63–89.

Mies, M. (2014). *Patriarchy and Accumulation on a World Scale.* London: Zed Books.

Mincer, J. (1958). Investment in Human Capital and Personal Income Distribution. *Journal of Political Economy*, 66(4): pp. 281–302.

Minsky, H. P. (1977). The Financial Instability Hypothesis. *Challenge*, 20(1): pp. 20–7.

Minsky, H. P. (1986). *Stabilizing an Unstable Economy.* New Haven: Yale University Press.

Mirchandani, K. (2004). Practices of Global Capital: Gaps, Cracks and Ironies in Transnational Call Centres in India. *Global Networks*, 4(4): pp. 355–73.

Mishel, L. and Bivens, J. (2017). *The Zombie Robot Argument Lurches On.* Washington DC: Economic Policy Institute: https://www.epi.org/files/pdf/126750.pdf.

Mishel, L. and Schieder, J. (2017). *CEO Pay Remains High Relative to Pay of Typical Workers and High-Wage Earners.* Washington DC: Economic Policy Institute: www.epi.org/files/pdf/130354.pdf.

Moffitt, R. A. (2003). The Negative Income Tax and the Evolution of US Welfare Policy. *Journal of Economic Perspectives*, 17(3): pp. 119–40.

Mohoun, S. (2006). Distributive Shares in the US Economy, 1964–2001. *Cambridge Journal of Economics*, 30(3): pp. 347–70.

Mohoun, S. (2014). Unproductive Labor in the U.S. Economy. *Review of Radical Political Economics*, 46(3): 355–79.

Mondragon Corporation (2016). Annual Report: https://www.mondragon-corporation.com/sobre-nosotros/magnitudes-economicas/informe-anual.

Mondragon Corporation (2017). Corporate Profile: https://www.mondragon-corporation.com/en/about-us/economic-and-financial-indicators/corporate-profile.

Moreno-Colom, S. (2017). The Gendered Division of Housework Time. *Time & Society*, 26(1): pp. 3–27.

Morris, D. Z. (2017). Robots are Moving in on E-Commerce Packing. *Fortune*: http://fortune.com/2017/07/23/ecommerce-packing-robots.

Moseley, F. (1997). The Rate of Profit and the Future of Capitalism. *Review of Radical Political Economics*, 29(4): pp. 23–41.

Mueller, G. and Plug, E. (2006). Estimating the Effect of Personality on Male and Female Earnings. *ILR Review*, 60(1): pp. 3–22.

Neeson, J. M. (2000). English Enclosures and British Peasants. *Jahrbuch für Wirtschaftsgeschichte*, 41: pp. 17–31.

Nelson, D. (1982). The Company Union Movement, 1900–1937. *Business History Review*, 56(3): pp. 335–57.

Nelson, J. (1996). *Feminism, Objectivity and Economics*. New York: Routledge.

Nelson, J. (1998). Labour, Gender and the Economic/Social Divide. *International Labour Review*, 137(1): pp. 33–46.

Nelson, R. (1964). Aggregate Production Functions and Medium-Range Growth Projections. *American Economic Review*, 54(5): pp. 575–606.

Neslen, A. (2015). EU Threatens Thailand with Trade Ban over Illegal Fishing. *Guardian*: https://www.theguardian.com/environment/2015/apr/21/eu-threatens-thailand-with-trade-ban-over-illegal-fishing.

Ngai, P. (2007). Gendering the Dormitory Labor System: Production, Reproduction, and Migrant Labor in South China. *Feminist Economics*, 13(3–4): pp. 239–58.

Nixon, R. (2013). Last of a Breed: Postal Workers Who Decipher Bad Addresses. *New York Times*: www.nytimes.com/2013/05/04/us/where-mail-with-illegible-addresses-goes-to-be-read.html.

Noble, D. F. (1984). *Forces of Production: A Social History of Machine Tool Automation*. New York: Alfred A. Knopf.

North, P. (2007). *Money and Liberation: The Micropolitics of Alternative Currency Movements*. Minneapolis: University of Minnesota Press.

Nuvolari, A. (2002). The "Machine Breakers" and the Industrial Revolution. *Journal of European Economic History*, 31(2): pp. 393–426.

OECD (2018). Employment by Activity (Indicator): https://data.oecd.org/emp/employment-by-activity.htm.

OECD.Stat (n.d.). Time Use database: https://stats.oecd.org/Index.aspx?datasetcode=TIME_USE.

Onaran, Ö., Stockhammer, E. and Grafl, L. (2011). Financialisation, Income Distribution and Aggregate Demand in the USA. *Cambridge Journal of Economics*, 35(4): pp. 637–61.

Osborne, M. (2008). Personality and the Intergenerational Transmission of Economic Status. In S. Bowles, H. Gintis and M. Osborne, eds., *Unequal Chances: Family Background and Economic Success*. Princeton University Press, pp. 208–31.

Oster, S. (2016). Inside One of the World's Most Secretive iPhone Factories. *Bloomberg News*: https://www.bloomberg.com/news/features/2016-04-24/inside-one-of-the-world-s-most-secretive-iphone-factories.

Osterman, P. (2006). The Wage Effects of High Performance Work Organization in Manufacturing. *ILR Review*, 59(2): pp. 187–204.

Osterman, P. (2018). In Search of the High Road. *ILR Review*, 71(1): pp. 3–34.

Otis, E. and Wu, T. (2018). The Deficient Worker: Skills, Identity, and Inequality in Service Employment. *Sociological Perspectives*, 61(5. DOI: 10.1177/0731121418766899

Ottaviano, G. I. and Peri, G. (2012). Rethinking the Effect of Immigration on Wages. *Journal of the European Economic Association*, 10(1): 152–97.

Pager, D., Bonikowski, B. and Western, B. (2009). Discrimination in a Low-Wage Labor Market. *American Sociological Review*, 74(5): pp. 777–99.

Pager, D., Western, B. and Sugie, N. (2009). Sequencing Disadvantage: Barriers to Employment Facing Young Black and White Men with Criminal Records. *Annals of the American Academy of Political and Social Science*, 623(1): pp. 195–213.

Palley, T. I. (2014). The Middle Class in Macroeconomics and Growth Theory. *Cambridge Journal of Economics*, 39(1): pp. 221–43.

Parker, M. and Slaughter, J. (1988). *Choosing Sides: Unions and the Team Concept*. Boston: South End Press.

Pasinetti, L. (1981). *Structural Change and Economic Growth*. Cambridge University Press.

Peck, J. and Theodore, N. (2012). Politicizing Contingent Work. *South Atlantic Quarterly*, 111(4): pp. 741–61.

Perry, M. (2016). Shackles and Dollars: Historians and Economists Clash over Slavery. *Chronicle of Higher Education*, 8 December: https://www.chronicle.com/article/ShacklesDollars/238598.

Phillips, A. and Taylor, B. (1980). Sex and Skill: Notes Towards a Feminist Economics. *Feminist Review*, 6: pp. 79–88.

Pietrykowski, B. (2015). Participatory Economic Research. *Review of Social Economy*, 73(3): pp. 242–62.

Pietrykowski, B. (2017a). Re-valuing Low Wage Work: Service Sector Skills and the Fight for 15. *Review of Radical Political Economics*, 49(1): pp. 5–329.

Pietrykowski, B. (2017b). The Return to Caring Skills. *Feminist Economics*, 23(4): pp. 32–61.

Piketty, T. (2014). *Capital in the Twentieth Century*. Cambridge, MA: Belknap Press of Harvard University Press.

Piketty, T. and Saez, E. (2014). Inequality in the Long Run. *Science*, 344(6186): pp. 838–43.

Piore, M. and Sabel, C. (1984). *The Second Industrial Divide*. New York: Basic Books.

Polachek, S. (1981). Occupational Self-Selection: A Human Capital Approach to Sex Differences in Occupational Structure. *Review of Economics and Statistics*, 63(1): pp. 63–9.

Polanyi, K. (1944). *The Great Transformation*. Boston: Beacon Press.

Poster, W. R. (2007). Who's on the Line? Indian Call Center Agents Pose as Americans for US-outsourced Firms. *Industrial Relations*, 46(2): pp. 271–304.

Preston, I. (2017). Fact Check: Does Immigration Have an Impact on Wages or Employment? *The Conversation*: http://theconversation.com/fact-check-does-immigration-have-an-impact-on-wages-or-employment-83666.

Pyper, D. and Brown, J. (2017). Zero-hours Contracts (House of Commons Library Briefing Paper No. 06553): http://research-briefings.files.parliament.uk/documents/SN06553/SN06553.pdf.

Rai, S. M., Hoskyns, C. and Thomas, D. (2014). Depletion: The Cost of Social Reproduction. *International Feminist Journal of Politics*, 16(1): pp. 86–105.

Raynolds, L. T. (2009). Mainstreaming Fair Trade Coffee. *World Development*, 37(6): pp. 1083–93.

Rehel, E. M. (2014). When Dad Stays Home Too. *Gender & Society*, 28(1): pp. 110–32.

Reich, R. (2016). Why We'll Need a Universal Basic Income: http://robertreich.org/post/151111696805.

Resnick, S. and Wolff, R. (1979). The Theory of Transitional Conjunctures and the Transition from Feudalism to Capitalism in Western Europe. *Review of Radical Political Economics*, 11(3): pp. 3–22.

Robeyns, I. (2003). Sen's Capability Approach and Gender Inequality. *Feminist Economics*, 9(2–3): pp. 61–92.

Rosenthal, C. (2016). Slavery's Scientific Management. In S. Beckert and S. Rockman, eds., *Slavery's Capitalism*. Philadelphia: University of Pennsylvania Press, pp. 62–86.

Royle, T. (2010). "Low-road Americanization" and the Global "McJob": A Longitudinal Analysis of Work, Pay and Unionization in the International Fast-food Industry. *Labor History*, 51(2): pp. 249–70.

Schechner, S. (2017). Meet Your New Boss: An Algorithm. *Wall Street Journal*: https://www.wsj.com/amp/articles/meet-your-new-boss-an-algorithm-1512910800.

Schroeder, K. (2006). A Feminist Examination of Community Kitchens in Peru and Bolivia. *Gender, Place and Culture*, 13(6): pp. 663–8.

Schultz, T. W. (1959). Investment in Man. *Social Service Review*, 33(2): pp. 109–17.

Schultz, T. W. (1961). Investment in Human Capital. *American Economic Review*, 51(1): pp. 1–17.

Schultz, T. W. (1962). Reflections on Investment in Man. *Journal of Political Economy*, 70(5, Part 2), pp. 1–8.

Sen, A. (1999). *Development as Freedom*. Oxford University Press.

Shantz, A., Alfes, K. and Truss, C. (2014). Alienation from Work: Marxist Ideologies and Twenty-First-Century Practice. *International Journal of Human Resource Management*, 25(18): pp. 2529–50.

Shierholz, H. (2010). Immigration and Wages (Economic Policy Institute Briefing Paper 255): https://www.epi.org/publication/bp255.

Silver, B. (2003). *Forces of Labor*. Cambridge University Press.

Simonazzi, A. (2008). Care Regimes and National Employment Models. *Cambridge Journal of Economics*, 33(2): pp. 211–32.

Slichter, S. (1920). Industrial Morale. *Quarterly Journal of Economics*, 35(1): pp. 36–60.

Smith, A. (1776). *The Wealth of Nations*: https://www.marxists.org/reference/archive/smith-adam/works/wealth-of-nations/book01/ch01.htm.

Smith, C. and Pun, N. (2006). The Dormitory Labour Regime in China as a Site for Control and Resistance. *International Journal of Human Resource Management*, 17(8): pp. 1456–70.

Smith, S. C. (2003). Network Externalities and Cooperative Networks. In L. Sun, ed., *Ownership and Governance of Enterprise*. London: Palgrave Macmillan, pp. 181–201.

Sodha, S. (2017). Is Finland's Basic Universal Income a Solution to Automation, Fewer Jobs and Lower Wages? *Guardian*: https://www.theguardian.com/society/2017/feb/19/basic-income-finland-low-wages-fewer-jobs.

Spectator (1866). Industrial Partnership: p. 569.

Spencer, D. A. (2000). Braverman and the Contribution of Labour Process Analysis to the Critique of Capitalist Production – Twenty-five Years On. *Work, Employment and Society*, 14(2): pp. 223–43.

Spencer, D. A. (2014). Developing an Understanding of Meaningful Work in Economics: The Case for a Heterodox Economics of Work. *Cambridge Journal of Economics*, 39(3): pp. 675–88.

Spencer-Wood, S. (2004). The Cambridge Cooperative Housekeeping Society. In K. S. Barile and J. C. Brandon, eds., *Household Chores and Household Choices*. Birmingham: University of Alabama Press, pp. 138–58.

Sperling, J. (2018). A New Zealand Company That Tested a Four-Day Work Week May Make It Permanent. *Fortune*: http://fortune.com/2018/07/23/perpetual-guardian-four-day-work-week.

Standing, G. (2011). *The Precariat: The New Dangerous Class*. London: Bloomsbury.

Standing, G. (2014). Understanding the Precariat through Labour and Work. *Development and Change*, 45(5): 963–80.

Steinberg, R. J. and Figart, D. M. (1999). Emotional Demands at Work. *Annals of the American Academy of Political and Social Science*, 561: pp. 177–91.

Steinmetz, G. (1994). Regulation Theory, Post-Marxism, and the New Social Movements. *Comparative Studies in Society and History*, 36(1): pp. 176–212.

Stilwell, F. (2016). Heterodox Economics or Political Economy? *Real-world Economics Review*, 74 (7 April 2016): pp. 42–8: www.paecon.net/PAEReview/issue74/Stilwell74.pdf.

Stockhammer, E. (2011). Wage-led Growth: An Introduction. *International Journal of Labour Research*, 3(2): pp. 167–87.

Stockhammer, E. and Stehrer, R. (2011). Goodwin or Kalecki in Demand? *Review of Radical Political Economics*, 43(4): pp. 506–22.

Streeck, W. (1995). Works Councils in Western Europe. In J. Rogers and W. Streeck, eds., *Works Councils: Consultation, Representation, and Cooperation in Industrial Relations*. University of Chicago Press, pp. 313–50.

Swider, S. (2015). Building China: Precarious Employment among Migrant Construction Workers. *Work, Employment and Society*, 29(1): pp. 41–59.

Szreter, S. and Mooney, G. (1998). Urbanization, Mortality, and the Standard of Living Debate: New Estimates of the Expectation of Life at Birth in Nineteenth-century British Cities. *Economic History Review*, 51(1): pp. 84–112.

Theodore, N., Valenzuela Jr., A. and Meléndez, E. (2009). Worker Centers: Defending Labor Standards for Migrant Workers in the Informal Economy. *International Journal of Manpower*, 30(5): pp. 422–36.

Thompson, E. P. (1966). *The Making of the English Working Class*. New York: Vintage.

Thompson, E. P. (1971). The Moral Economy of the English Crowd in the Eighteenth Century. *Past & Present*, (50): pp. 76–136.

University of Michigan (2007). Time, Money and Who Does the Laundry? (Institute for Social Research, Research Report 4): pp. 1–2: https://deepblue.lib.umich.edu/bitstream/handle/2027.42/61984/chores.pdf;jsessionid=7001D71465DCFA4C78E604E121417010.

Van Parijs, P. (2004). Basic Income: A Simple and Powerful Idea for the Twenty-First Century. *Politics & Society*, 32(1): pp. 7–39.

Vestbro, D. U. (1997). Collective Housing in Scandinavia. *Journal of Architectural and Planning Research*, 14(4): pp. 329–42.

Vestbro, D. U. and Horelli, L. (2012). Design for Gender Equality. *Built Environment*, 38(3): pp. 315–35.

Vivarelli, M. (2014). Innovation, Employment and Skills in Advanced and Developing Countries: A Survey of Economic Literature. *Journal of Economic Issues*, 48(1): pp. 123–54.

Voss, K. and Sherman, R. (2000). Breaking the Iron Law of Oligarchy: Union Revitalization in the American Labor Movement. *American Journal of Sociology*, 106(2): pp. 303–49.

Wadiwel, D. J. (2016). Do Fish Resist? *Cultural Studies Review*, 22(1): pp. 196–242.

Warhurst, C. and Nickson, D. (2007). Employee Experience of Aesthetic Labour in Retail and Hospitality. *Work, Employment and Society*, 21(1): pp. 103–20.

Waring, M. (1990). *If Women Counted: A New Feminist Economics*. San Francisco: Harper & Row.

Webbink, E., Smits, J. and de Jong, E. (2012). Hidden Child Labor: Determinants of Housework and Family Business Work of Children in 16 Developing Countries. *World Development*, 40(3): pp. 631–42.

Weeks, K. (2011). *The Problem with Work: Feminism, Marxism, Antiwork Politics, and Postwork Imaginaries*. Durham: Duke University Press.

Weeks, K. (2014). The Problems with Work. *New Labor Forum*, 23(2): pp. 10–12.

Weil, D. (2014). *The Fissured Workplace*. Cambridge, MA: Harvard University Press.

Weissmann, J. (2013). McDonald's Can't Figure Out How its Workers Survive on Minimum Wage. *The Atlantic*: https://www.theatlantic.com/business/archive/2013/07/mcdonalds-cant-figure-out-how-its-workers-survive-on-minimum-wage.

Whyte, W. F. and Whyte, K. K. (1988). *Making Mondragon*. Ithaca, NY: ILR Press.

Williams, C. L. and Connell, C. (2010). "Looking Good and Sounding Right": Aesthetic Labor and Social Inequality in the Retail Industry. *Work and Occupations*, 37(3): pp. 349–77.

Wolfson, M. and Kotz, D. M. (2010). A Reconceptualization of Social Structure of Accumulation Theory. In T. McDonough, M. Reich and D. M. Kotz, eds., *Contemporary Capitalism and its Crises*. Cambridge University Press, pp. 72–90.

World Bank (2011). *World Development Report 2012: Gender Equality and Development*. Washington DC: World Bank Group.

Wright, E. O. (2006). Basic Income as a Socialist Project. *Basic Income Studies*, 1(1): pp. 1–11.

Zalewski, D. A. and Whalen, C. J. (2010). Financialization and Income Inequality: A Post Keynesian Institutionalist Analysis. *Journal of Economic Issues*, 44(3): pp. 757–77.

Index